The Battles for Empire
Volume 1

The Battles for Empire
Volume 1

Battles of the British Army through the

Victorian Age, 1824–1857

ILLUSTRATED

Robert Blackwood

and

Bruce Hay

LEONAUR

The Battles for Empire
Volume 1
Battles of the British Army through the Victorian Age, 1824-1857
by Robert Blackwood and Bruce Hay

ILLUSTRATED

FIRST EDITION

Leonaur is an imprint of Oakpast Ltd
Copyright in this form © 2023 Oakpast Ltd

ISBN: 978-1-916535-02-2 (hardcover)
ISBN: 978-1-916535-03-9 (softcover)

http://www.leonaur.com

Publisher's Notes

Contents

CHAPTER 1

The Battle of Kemmendine: 1824

In 1824 the British were forced into a war with the kingdom of Burmah. The war, however, was not of our seeking; we were forced into it. The Burmese a few years previously had taken forcible possession of the province of Assam, which was soon followed by parties of these people committing serious devastations within British territory, burning a number of villages, plundering and murdering the inhabitants, or carrying them off as slaves. At the same time an island in the Brahmaputra, on which the British flag had been erected, was invaded, the flag was thrown down, and an armed force collected to maintain the insult.

To meet these difficulties, and to strengthen their eastern frontier, the British Government resolved upon occupying Kachar, with the more important province of Manipur, which had long ago requested the protection of the British against the tyranny of the Burmahs. Active hostilities had by this time broken out at the boundaries.

The British asked for a commission of inquiry and settlement to be appointed. This request was answered by an attack upon, and the capture of the British post of Shahpuri, an affair that was attended with considerable loss of life; and which was followed by a menacing letter from the Rajah of Arracan, to the effect that unless the British Government submitted quietly it would be followed by the like forcible seizure of the cities of Dacca and Moorshedabad.

The British now called upon the court of Ava to disavow the proceedings of its officers in Arracan. This last act of mistaken and temporising policy had no other effect than that of confirming the court of Ava in their confident expectation of annexing the eastern provinces of Bengal if not of expelling the British from India altogether.

There followed several minor engagements, and in May of 1824 the British forces got possession of Rangoon after a trifling resistance.

The Kemmendine Attack

The troops were posted in the immense *pagoda* of the town, where many unfortunate prisoners were discovered, forgotten by the Burmahs in the confusion of their retreat.

Rumours of the arrival of Bandoola with the main body of his grand army, reached Rangoon early in November, 1824, and towards the end of the month an intercepted dispatch from Bandoola to the ex-governor of Martaban, announced his having left Prome, at the head of an invincible army, with horses and elephants, and every kind of stores, to capture or expel the British from Rangoon. Every arrangement was then made to give him a warm reception.

The post at Kemmendine was strongly occupied and supported on the river, by His Majesty's sloop *Sophie*, commanded by Captain Ryves, and a strong division of gunboats; this post was of great importance in preventing the enemy from attacking Rangoon by water, or launching from a convenient distance the many fire rafts he had prepared for effecting the destruction of our shipping.

On the 30th of November the Burmese Army was assembled in the extensive forest in front of the *pagoda*, and his line extending from the river above Kemmendine in a semi-circular direction towards Puzendown, might be distinguished by a curved line of smoke rising above the trees from the bivouacs of the different corps. During the following night, the low continued murmur and hum of voices proceeding from the Burmese encampment, suddenly ceased, and was succeeded by the distant, but gradually approaching sounds of a multitude in slow and silent movement through the woods.

The enemy's masses had approached to the very edge of the jungle, within musket shot of the *pagoda*, apparently in readiness to rush from their cover to the assault at break of day. Towards morning, however, the woods resounded with the blows of the felling axe and hammer, and with the crash of falling trees, leaving the British for some time in doubt whether or not the noise was intended as a ruse to draw attention from the front, or whether the Burmese commanders had resolved to proceed with their usual slow and systematic measures of attack.

Day had scarcely dawned on the 1st of December, when hostilities commenced with a heavy fire of musketry and cannon at Kemmendine, the reduction of that place being a preliminary to any general attack on our line. The fire continued long and animated, and from the commanding situation of the Great Pagoda, though nearly two miles distant from the scene of action, we could distinctly hear

9

the yells and shouts of the infuriated assailants, occasionally answered by the hearty cheers of the British seamen as they poured in their heavy broadsides upon the resolute and persevering masses.

In the course of the forenoon Burmese columns were perceived on the west side of the river, marching across the plain of Dalla, towards Rangoon. They were formed in five or six different divisions, and moved with great regularity, led by numerous chiefs on horseback, their gilt umbrellas glittering in the rays of the sun, with a sufficiently formidable and imposing effect, at a distance that prevented our perceiving anything motley or mobbish, which might have been found in a closer inspection of these warlike legions.

On reaching the bank of the river opposite to Rangoon, the men of the leading Burmese division, laying aside their arms, commenced entrenching and throwing up batteries for the destruction of the shipping, while the main body disappeared in a jungle in the rear, where they began stockading and establishing their camp, gradually reinforcing the front line as the increasing extent of the batteries and entrenchments permitted. Later in the day, several heavy columns were observed issuing from the forest, about a mile in front of the east face of the Great Pagoda, with flags and banners flying in profusion.

Their march was directed along a gently sloping woody ridge towards Rangoon; the different corps successively taking up their ground along the ridge, soon assumed the appearance of a complete line, extending from the forest in front of the *pagoda* to within long gunshot distance of the town, and resting on the river at Puzendown, which was strongly occupied by cavalry and infantry; these formed the left wing of the Burmese Army. The centre, or the continuation of the line from the Great Pagoda up to Kemmendine, where it again rested on the river, was posted in so thick a forest as to defy all conjecture as to its strength or situation; but we were well aware that the principal force occupied the jungle in the immediate vicinity of the *pagoda*, which was naturally considered as the key to our position, and upon which the great effort would accordingly be made.

When this singular and presumptuous formation was completed, the soldiers of the left columns also laying aside their spears and muskets, commenced operations with their entrenching tools, with such goodwill and activity that in the course of a couple of hours their line had wholly disappeared, and could only be traced by a parapet of new earth gradually increasing in height, and assuming such forms as the skill and science of the engineer suggested.

The moving masses which had so lately attracted our anxious attention, had sunk into the ground; and to anyone who had not witnessed the whole scene, the existence of these subterraneous legions would not have been credited; the occasional movement of a chief with his gilt *chattah* (umbrella) from place to place superintending the progress of their labour, was the only thing that now attracted notice. By a distant observer, the hills, covered with mounds of earth would have been taken for anything rather than the approaches of an attacking army.

In the afternoon, His Majesty's thirteenth regiment, and the eighteenth Madras Native Infantry, under Major Sale, were ordered to move rapidly forward upon the busily employed and too confident enemy.

As was expected, they were quite unprepared for a sudden visit, not expecting that we would venture to act on the offensive against so numerous a body.

They had scarcely noticed the advance of our troops when they were upon them, nor could the fire which they opened upon their assailants check their advance. Having forced a passage through the entrenchments and taken the enemy in flank, the British detachment drove the whole line from their cover with considerable loss; and having destroyed as many of their arms and tools as they could find, retired unmolested before the numerous bodies which were now forming on every side around them.

The trenches were found to be a succession of holes, capable of containing two men each, and excavated so as to afford shelter both from the fire of their opponents and from the weather; even a shell falling into the trench could only prove fatal to two men. As it is not the Burmese custom to relieve their troops in making these approaches, each hole had in it a sufficient supply of rice, water, and even fuel for its inmates; under the excavated bank a bed of straw or brushwood was placed in which one man could sleep whilst his comrade watched.

The Burmese in the course of the evening, re-occupied their trenches, recommencing their labours as if nothing untoward had occurred. Their commander, however, took the precaution of bringing forward a strong corps of reserve to the verge of the forest, from which his left wing had issued, to protect it from any future interruptions in its operations.

During the day repeated attacks on Kemmendine had been made and repulsed; but it was not until darkness set in that the last desperate effort of the day was made, to obtain possession of that post. Already had the fatigued soldiers laid down to rest, when all of a sudden, the heavens and country round became brilliantly illuminated, caused by the flames of several immense fire-rafts, floating down the river towards Rangoon.

Scarcely had the blaze of light appeared when incessant rolls of musketry and peals of cannon were heard from Kemmendine. The Burmese had launched the fire-rafts into the stream with the first of the ebb tide, in the hope of forcing the vessels from their stations off the place, and they were followed by war-boats ready to take advantage of the confusion likely to ensue, should any of the vessels have caught fire. The skill and intrepidity, however, of British seamen proved more than a match for the numbers and arts of the enemy; they grappled the blazing rafts, and conducted them past the shipping or ran them ashore upon the bank.

On the land side the enemy was equally unsuccessful, being again repulsed with great loss in the most resolute attempt they had yet made to reach the interior of the fort.

These fire-rafts, upon examination, were found to be of ingenious construction, as well as formidable; they were made of bamboos firmly wrought together, between every two or three rows of which a line of earthen jars of considerable size, filled with petroleum, or earth-oil and cotton, were securely fixed.

With the possession of Kemmendine, the enemy would have launched these destructive rafts into the stream from a point which would have caused them to reach our shipping in the crowded harbour; but so long as we retained possession of that post, they were obliged to launch them higher up, and the setting of the current carried them, after passing the shipping on the station, upon a projecting point of land where they almost invariably grounded; this circumstance doubtless greatly increased Bandoola's anxiety to drive the British from such an important position.

On the morning of the second, at daylight, the enemy were seen still actively at work on every part of their line, and to have completely entrenched themselves upon some high and open ground, within musket shot distance of the north face of the Great Pagoda, from which it was also separated by a considerable tank, named by the Rangoon settlers, the Scotch tank, probably on account of the sulphureous qualities of its water.

In the spirited encounters which the enemy's near approach gave rise to, it was highly gratifying to observe the undaunted bearing of the British soldier, in the midst of countless numbers of the enemy who were not to be driven from their ground by the united fire of musketry and cannon. In the imagined security of their cover they firmly maintained themselves, and returned our fire; and it was only at the intrepid and decisive charge that they quailed to the courage of the European, and declined meeting him hand to hand.

During the third and fourth, the enemy continued their approaches upon every part of our position with indefatigable assiduity. At the Great Pagoda they had now reached the margin of the tank, and kept up a constant fire upon our barracks, saluting with a dozen muskets everyone who showed his head above the ramparts, and when nothing better could be done, expending both round and grape shot in vain attempts to strike the British ensign which proudly waved high upon their sacred temple.

On the side of Rangoon, they had approached near enough to fire an occasional gun upon the town, while they maintained incessant warfare with two small posts in its front to which they were now so near as to keep their garrisons constantly on the alert, in the expectation of being attacked.

From the entrenchments on the opposite side of the river an incessant fire was kept up day and night upon our shipping, which were all anchored as near as possible to the Rangoon side, with the exception of one or two armed vessels which still kept the middle of the stream, and returned the fire of the enemy.

At Kemmendine peace was seldom maintained above two hours at any time; but the little garrison (composed of the 26th Madras Native Infantry, and a European detachment), though worn out with fatigue and want of rest, undauntedly received, and successfully repulsed, every successive attack of the fresh troops brought to bear upon them.

The *sepoys*, with unwearied constancy and the noblest feeling, even declined leaving their post, or laying aside their muskets for the purpose of cooking, lest the enemy should obtain any advantage, and for several days felt contented with little else than dry rice for food.

The material and warlike stores of the enemy's left wing being now brought forward from the jungle to the entrenchments, and completely within our reach, and their threatening vicinity to the town creating some uneasiness for the safety of our military stores, which were all lodged in that ill-protected and highly-combustible assemblage of huts and wooden houses, the British general, Sir Archibald Campbell, determined upon attacking decisively that portion of the opposing army.

On the morning of the 5th, two columns of attack, consisting of detachments from different regiments, were formed for the purpose. One column consisting of eight hundred men, under Major Sale of the 13th regiment, and the other of five hundred men under Major Walker of the Madras Army. Major Sale was directed to attack the centre of the enemy's line, and Major Walker to advance from the post in front of the town, and to attack vigorously on that side; and a troop of dragoons, which had only been landed on the previous day was added to the first column, ready to take advantage of the retreat, of the enemy across the open ground to the jungle.

According to the arrangement, early on that morning, Captain Chads, the naval commander, proceeded up to Puzendown Creek, within gunshot of the rear of the enemy's line, with the man-of-war boats and part of the flotilla, and commenced a heavy cannonade upon the nearest entrenchments, attracting the enemy's chief attention to that point, until the preconcerted signal for attack was made, when both columns moved off together; but from some obstacle in the ground Major Walker's party first reached its destined point, and made a spirited assault on the lines.

The enemy made a stout resistance, and Major Walker and many of his brave and gallant comrades fell in the advance to the first entrenchment, which was finally carried at the point of the bayonet, and the enemy driven from trench to trench, till this part of the field presented the appearance of a total rout.

The other column now commencing its attack in front, quickly forced the centre, and the whole Burmese left wing, entrenched upon the plain was broken and dispersed, flying in hundreds, or assembled in confused and detached parties, or else maintaining a useless and disjointed resistance at different parts of the works, to which our troops had not yet penetrated.

The two British columns now forming a junction, pursued, and drove the defendants from every part of their works into the jungle, leaving the ground behind them covered with the dead and wounded, with all their guns and entrenching tools, and a great number of small arms; while the judgment, celerity, and spirit with which the attack was made had taken the enemy so completely by surprise, that our troops suffered comparatively but little loss.

The 6th was spent by Bandoola in rallying his defeated left; but it appeared to be still far from his intention to give up the contest on account of the failures and defeats he had already sustained. In front of the Great Pagoda his troops, still laboured with the greatest zeal in their approaches upon our position, and this part of his line had been strongly reinforced by the troops which had been driven from the plain on the preceding day.

The morning of the 7th was fixed upon for bringing matters to a crisis at this point, and four columns of attack, composed of detachments, were early formed under the superintendence of the commander of the forces, in readiness to move from the *pagoda* and assail the entrenchments on both flanks and in the centre. Before the troops advanced, a severe cannonade was opened from many pieces of heavy ordnance, brought up from the river, and placed in battery for defending this important post. This the enemy stood with much firmness, and returned it with a constant, though unequal, fire of musketry, *jingals*, and light artillery.

While the firing continued, the columns of attack were already in motion towards their several points; and when it ceased, the left corps, under Colonel Mallet, was seen debouching from the jungle upon the enemy's right; the right column, under Colonel Brodie, Madras Army, in like manner advancing on the left; and the two central columns, one under Colonel Parlby of the Madras Army, and the other commanded by Captain Wilson, of the 38th regiment, descending the stairs from the north gate of the *pagoda* and filing up towards the centre of the position, by either side of the tank before alluded to, as partly covering the entrenchments on this side.

The appearance of our troops at the same moment upon so many different points seemed to paralyse the Burmese Army, but they were not long in recovering from their momentary panic, when they opened a heavy and well-sustained fire upon our troops; and it was not until a decided charge was made, and our troops actually in the trenches, that the enemy finally gave way, and they were precipitately driven from their numerous works, curiously shaped, and strengthened by many strange contrivances, into the thick forest in their rear.

There, all pursuit was necessarily given up; our limited numbers, exhausted by seven days of watching and hard service, were unequal to the fatigue; though even when our men were fresh, the enemy could always baffle their pursuit in a country which afforded them so many facilities for escaping. Upon the ground the enemy left a great number of dead, who seemed generally from their stout and athletic forms, to have been their best troops. Their bodies had each a charm of some description, in which the brave deceased had no doubt trusted for protection, but in this case, they seemed to have lost any virtue ever possessed by them. In the entrenchments were found scaling-ladders, and every preparation for carrying the *pagoda* by storm.

No time was lost in completing the rout of the Burmese Army, and on the evening of the 7th, a body of troops from His Majesty's Eighty-Ninth regiment, and the Forty-Third Madras Native Infantry, under Colonel Parlby, were in readiness to embark from Rangoon as soon as the tide served, for the purpose of crossing the river and driving the enemy from their entrenchments at Dalla. The night, fortunately, was dark, and the troops were got over unperceived by the enemy. No shot was fired, nor alarm given, until the British troops had actually entered the Burmese entrenchments, and commenced firing at random among the noisy groups which they now heard all around them, but the risk of injuring each other in the dark made it advisable to desist.

Parties were sent to occupy various parts of the works, which a previous acquaintance with the ground enabled them to accomplish with but little opposition or loss. On the approach of daylight next morning, they found themselves in full and undisturbed possession of the whole position, with all the guns and stores of this portion of the Burmese Army, the remains of which were perceived during the whole day, retracing their steps across the plain of Dalla, with more expedition and less pomp than they had exhibited but seven days before, when they traversed the same plain "in all the pomp and circumstance of glorious war."

Every gun they had, and the whole materiel of the army, fell into the hands of the conquerors. Desertions and the dispersion of entire corps, followed the defeat, so that in the course of a few days the haughty Bandoola, who so boasted of driving the rebel strangers into the sea, found himself completely foiled in all his plans, humbled, and surrounded by a beaten army, which he proudly called "invincible," alike afraid of the consequences of a final retreat, and of another meeting with an adversary who had taught him such a severe lesson!

CHAPTER 2

The Battle of Melloone: 1825

After various successes, Sir Archibald Campbell was enabled to make his arrangements for an advance upon the Burmese capital. The distance from Prome to Ava may be estimated at three hundred miles, and although the roads and country upwards are generally more advantageous for military operations than those in the lower provinces, we had still much toil and labour to anticipate before the army could arrive in the open plains of Upper Ava.

The commissariat was conducted by natives, who even volunteered their services as drivers to the foot artillery, and on various occasions did not flinch from exposing themselves to the fire of their countrymen, expressing much pleasure at the precision with which the guns to which they were attached were directed by their new allies.

The officers, instead of walking, had now the luxury of being mounted on Pegu ponies, and they commenced the second campaign in good health, and in comparative comfort.

On the 9th of December, the first division began its march through very bad roads for guns and carriages. On the 10th, marched to Wattygoon, and found the ten stockades which had formerly been attacked, unoccupied by the enemy. The position had been chosen with wonted judgment of the Burmhan engineers, having two sides protected by a deep morass; a jungle covered the approach on the third side, the rear alone was open ground, and the only point from which the works could be successfully assailed.

Next day the army marched five miles over a thickly-enclosed country, without any appearance of houses or population. The following day other five miles were done over almost impassable roads through recent rains, and with very bad camping ground, where cholera made its appearance. After two weeks of most trying and difficult marching, the army, on the 25th, reached Longhee, and on the 26th moved onward ten miles, when a flag of truce arrived from Melloone, announcing the appearance of a commissioner, named Kolein Mengie, with full powers from the king to conclude a treaty of peace.

On the 27th an answer was returned, stating the concurrence of the British commissioners, and the division continued its advance, encamping on the banks of the Irrawaddy, about four miles below Melloone, where we were joined by the flotilla, and from whence could be seen the entrenched camp of the enemy.

The army had now marched one hundred and forty miles from Prome, and had not met with one inhabitant; and so completely had the enemy laid the line of our advance waste, that we were not able to obtain a single day's supply in a country but lately abounding in cattle. A fruitless negotiation was entered into at Melloone; our two officers then declared that on their departure from the place the British commander would commence offensive operations.

On the 29th the division again moved forward, and in two hours reached Patanagoh, a town upon the river, directly opposite to Melloone. The River Irrawaddy at this place is 600 yards broad, and the fortifications of Melloone, built upon the face of a sloping hill, lay fully exposed to view, within good practice distance of our artillery. The principal stockade appeared to be a square of about a mile, filled with men, and mounting a considerable number of guns, especially on the water-face; and the whole position, consisting of a succession of stockades, might extend nearly two miles along the beach.

In the centre of the great stockade, a handsome new gilt *pagoda* was observed, which had been raised to the memory of Maha Bandoola, to stimulate the present leaders to imitate his example at Donoobew, when he preferred death to quitting his post. On our arrival before the place, the Burmese discontinued their labours at their defences, and stood in groups gazing at us as we formed on the opposite bank. Under the stockade, a large fleet of war-boats, commissariat boats, and other craft, lay at anchor.

The army had not long reached our ground, when the loud clash of gongs, drums, and other warlike instruments drew our attention to the works of the enemy; crowds of boatmen were seen with their short oars across their shoulders, running to the beach, and every boat was speedily manned, and in motion up the river. The steam vessel and flotilla had been detained below the enemy's position, by the intricacy of the channel, and until protecting batteries could be formed to keep down the fire of the works along the beach, it became necessary to

18

adopt other measures to prevent the escape of the boats; accordingly, the artillery was ordered to fire upon them, which soon checked their progress, the boatmen either jumping into the river, or returning in the utmost haste to their former situation.

In the meantime, the flotilla, led by the *Diana* steam vessel, had got under way, when the firing commenced, and was now seen passing close under the enemy's works, without a shot being fired on either side. On reaching the principal stockade, two gilt war-boats pushing off from the shore, received the *Diana* with every honour, and escorted the squadron at some distance above the place, cutting off all retreat from it by water. Such unequivocal marks of a desire to prevent further hostility were immediately favourably accepted, and during the forenoon a truce was concluded and arrangements made for entering upon negotiations on the following day.

The Burmese chiefs, at their own request, were allowed to moor a large accommodation boat in the middle of the river, between the two armies, as the place of conference; and two o'clock on the 1st of January was fixed for the first meeting with the new delegate from Ava. Accordingly, the commissioners of both nations entered the conference nearly at the same time, the Kee Wongee, as joint commissioner, and most of the chiefs we had met at Neoun-benzeik, with several others, accompanied His Majesty's deputy, Kolein Menghi.

The countenance of this personage, apparently withered and shrivelled up by age, was strongly expressive of low cunning and dissimulation; at a first glance he might have passed for a man of seventy, but the vivacity and keenness of a pair of sharp grey eyes reduced it some dozen years. Though splendidly dressed, he presented a vulgar contrast to the easy and dignified demeanour of Kee Wongee, who had a frank and open countenance.

When seated in the boat, the business was opened with much solemnity. In answer to the demand of one *crore* of *rupees* (which, valuing the *rupee* at two shillings, the then rate of exchange, amounted to one million sterling), Kolein Menghi pleaded the expense they had been put to, by raising so many armies, which had drained their treasury, saying it was cruel to exact such a sum, which they could not pay, offering to allow the British to cut down their fine trees, adding, "we could, perhaps, in one year, by economy, give you a million baskets of rice, but we do not grow *rupees*, and have no way of procuring such a sum as you require." The cession of Arracan, and the restoration of Cassay to its legitimate owner, Gumbheer Sing, was disputed by

Kolein Menghi.

After four meetings, and prolonged discussions, in which the Burmese commissioners displayed great meanness, having had recourse to downright begging, after cunning and art had failed, the treaty was at last signed, fifteen days (to the 18th) being allowed for obtaining the ratification of the King of Ava and the performance of all preliminaries, *viz.*, the delivery of all prisoners, and the payment of the first money instalment.

During this interval the two camps carried on a friendly intercourse, and which was occasionally interrupted by the enemy working at, and strengthening his defences, especially during the night. Remonstrances were of course made, but the Burmese chiefs, with a dexterous cunning, parried the accusation of insincerity, at the same time expatiating on the blessings of peace between the "two great nations." At length, on the 17th, a deputation of three officers of state (two Attawoons and a Woondock) visited the British commissioners, pretending to account for the non-arrival of the ratified treaty, prisoners, etc., by some unforeseen accident, declaring that they had not heard from Ava since the treaty was sent there.

The commissioners, however, well knew that boats were in daily communication with Ava, and this glaring falsehood put them on their guard against suspected treachery. Having in the meantime made other offers to the British commissioners, which were all refused most decidedly, they at last entreated a delay of five or six days. This was also refused, and at the same time they were told to communicate to the prince and the two Wongees, the final resolution of the British commissioners; that if they evacuated Melloone in thirty-six hours, and continued retiring with their forces before the British Army upon Ava, hostilities would not be recommenced, and the march would be suspended, as soon as the ratified treaty should be received from Ava.

This proposition being peremptorily rejected, and the armistice being ended on the 18th, three officers were sent over to Melloone, who gave formal information that no farther forbearance or concession could be made, that having acted such a deceitful part, ample satisfaction should be demanded and enforced. The hour of twelve at night was named as the last hour of peace, and no satisfaction having been offered by these treacherous chiefs, the British at the specified hour began with alacrity to prepare for the attack by throwing up batteries opposite to the chosen points of attack in the stockade, which was within gunshot range of our bank of the river; the heavy ordnance was landed from the flotilla during the night, and by ten o'clock next morning, twenty-eight pieces of artillery were in battery, and prepared to open upon the defences of the enemy.

Shortly after eleven o'clock, the fire from our batteries began, and continued incessant and with much effect for nearly two hours, by which time the troops intended for the assault were embarked in the boats, under the superintendence of Captain Chads, as senior naval officer, at some distance above the place, in order to ensure their not being carried past it by the force of the stream. The first Bengal brigade, consisting of His Majesty's 13th and 38th regiments, under Lieutenant-Colonel Slade, was directed to land below the stockade, and attack it by the south-west angle, while three brigades were ordered to land above the place, and after carrying some outworks, to attack it by the northern face.

Notwithstanding every previous arrangement, and the utmost exertion of every one employed, the current, together with a strong northerly wind, carried the first brigade under all the fire of the place, to its destined point of attack, before the other brigades could reach the opposite shore, and being soon formed under the partial cover of a shelving bank, without waiting for the co-operation of the other troops, led by Lieutenant-Colonel Frith (Lieutenant-Colonel Slade having been wounded in the boats), moved forward to the assault with a steadiness and regularity that must have struck awe into the minds of their opponents, and in a very short time entered the place by escalade, and established themselves in the interior of the works.

A prouder or more gratifying sight has seldom, perhaps, been witnessed, than this mere handful of gallant fellows driving a dense multitude of from ten to fifteen thousand armed men before them, from works of such strength that even Memiaboo, contrary to all custom, did not think it necessary to leave them until the troops were in the act of carrying them. The other brigades cutting in upon the enemy's retreat, completed their defeat, and they were driven with severe loss from all their stockades, leaving the whole of their artillery and military stores in possession of the British.

In the house of Prince Memiaboo, was found cash to the amount of from thirty to forty thousand *rupees*; the whole of his stud was also made a prize of. The perfidy of the prince, the Wongees, and the government was now clearly demonstrated, as both the Burmese and British copies of the treaty were found in the house, in the same condition as when signed and sealed on the 3rd instant, along with all the other documents that were executed at Neoun-benzeik; besides several other papers written by a priest styled the Raja Goroo, a spiritual friend and the counsellor of the King of Ava, who had been for some time in the British lines, and had been employed to convey a pacific message to His Burmhan Majesty.

Memiaboo and his discomfited army retired with all possible haste from the scene of his disaster; while the British commander made instant preparation to follow him. Before, however, commencing his march, he despatched a messenger with the unratified treaty to the Kee Wongee, as well to show the Burmese chiefs that their perfidy was exposed, as to give them the opportunity of still ratifying their engagements, merely stating in a note to the Wongee that in the hurry of his departure from Melloone, he had forgotten a document which he might now find more useful and acceptable to his government than they had considered it a few days previously.

The Wongee and his colleague politely returned their best, thanks for the paper, but observed that the same hurry, which caused the loss of the treaty, had compelled them to leave behind also a large sum of money, which they likewise much regretted, and which they felt confident the British general only waited the opportunity of returning!

CHAPTER 3

The Battle of Pagahm–Mew: 1825

On the 25th of January, the British Army again moved forward, the road still worse; and on the 31st, the headquarters were at Zaynan-gheoun, or Earth-oil-Creek.

The capture of Melloone, as was expected, alarmed the King of Ava, who in order to avert greater calamity, sent Dr. Price, an American missionary, and Assistant-Surgeon Sandford, of the royal regiment, who had been taken prisoner some months before, on his parole of honour to return to Ava, accompanied by four prisoners returned by the king as a compliment. The poor fellows made a miserable appearance, never having been shaved, or had their hair cut since taken. They were sent to state the king's wish for peace, and to learn the most favourable terms. The answer varied but little from those formerly offered at Melloone; but the British general acceded to the request not to pass Pagahm-mew for twelve days, to allow time for transmitting the money from Ava.

On the next morning, the two delegates set off for Ava, Surgeon Price full of hope that he would return in a few days to conclude the peace. From the returned prisoners information was obtained which very clearly showed the hostile intentions of the King of Ava twelve months before hostilities commenced, when he was making arrangements for the conquest of Bengal.

Maha Bandoola was the grand projector, who told His Majesty that with 100,000 men he would pledge himself to succeed. So confident was this boaster, that when he marched into Arracan, he was provided with golden fetters, in which the Governor-General of India was to be led into Ava as a captive.

On coming near to Pagahm-mew, rumours were afloat that the Court of Ava were levying fresh troops; forty thousand had been induced by large promises to come forward, under the patriotic title of

23

Gong-to-doo, or Retrievers of the King's Glory! This army was placed under the command of a savage warrior, styled Nee-Woon-Breen, which has been variously translated as Prince of Darkness, King of Hell, and Prince of the Setting Sun. On the 8th, when within a day's march of Pagahm-mew, certain intelligence was obtained that the Nee-Woon-Breen was prepared to meet the British force under the walls of that city.

On the 9th of February, the British column moved forward in order of attack, reduced considerably under two thousand men by the absence of two brigades. The advance guard was met in the jungle by strong bodies of skirmishers, and after maintaining a running fight for several miles, the column debouching into the open country, discovered the Burmese Army nearly 20,000 strong, drawn up in an inverted crescent, the wings of which threatened the little body of assailants on either flank.

Undismayed, however, by the strong position of this formidable body, the British commander boldly pushed forward for their centre. The attack was so vigorous that the enemy gave way, being completely divided into two; the divided wings had much to do to reach a second line of redoubts under the walls of Pagahm-mew, which had been prepared in anticipation of such an untoward event.

The British column lost no time, but followed the retreating enemy so rapidly that they had not time for rallying in their works, into which they were closely followed and again routed with great loss; hundreds jumped into the river, and there perished. The whole of this remaining force, with the exception of two or three thousand men, dispersed, leaving the conquerors in quiet possession of their well-merited conquest.

The unfortunate commander, Nee-Woon-Breen, on reaching Ava, was very cruelly put to death, by the king's command.

On the evening of the 13th, Mr. Price and Mr. Sandford, now liberated, arrived in camp, when Mr. Price announced that the king and court had consented to yield to the formerly proposed terms, as they now saw that further opposition was of no avail. Yet the prisoners were not returned, nor was the first instalment, being twenty-five *lacs* of *rupees*, forthcoming. However, they said that everything was ready to be delivered, only the king hesitated letting the cash go out of his possession, apprehending that we should, notwithstanding, still hold his country, which he would assuredly do in like circumstances, he was anxious, therefore, to learn if we could be persuaded to accept of six *lacs* of *rupees* now, and the remaining nineteen *lacs* on the arrival of the army at Prome. To all this was added an earnest request that in any case the army might not come nearer to the capital.

A positive refusal to all this was returned, and on the following morning Mr. Price returned to Ava, assuring us of his return in a few days with some of the Burmhan ministers, in order to make a final settlement.

The army continuing to advance, was met at Yandaboo, only forty-five miles from Ava, by Mr. Price, and two ministers of state; accompanied by the prisoners, and the stipulated sum of twenty-five *lacs* of *rupees*. These ambassadors were empowered to state the unreserved acquiescence of their master, who had authorised them by his royal sign *manuel*, to accept of and sign such terms aa we might propose.

On the 24th of February the treaty was, for the second time, settled, and finally signed; the Burmese Government, at the same time, engaging to furnish boats for the conveyance of a great part of the force to Rangoon.

Here this war may be considered as ended; a war into which the government of India had been compelled to enter; and it was of a more protracted and serious character than any in which our eastern government had been engaged for many years. It was further distinguished from all others by the persevering obstinacy of the enemy, and the many difficulties, obstacles, and privations with which the British force had to contend for such a length of time.

Men and officers felt proud in having at last compelled our stubborn foe to sign a peace, honourable and advantageous to the British, as it was humiliating and inglorious to the Court of Ava; proud that the utmost wishes of our government had been realised, and the service they had been employed on, completed to the fullest extent.

CHAPTER 4

The First Afghan War, 1838-1842

By Captain Bruce Hay, p.s.c., Queen's Own Corps of Guides

England and Russia had for some years previously been striving for the paramount influence in Afghanistan, and in 1838 Russia made the first attempt to enter into an alliance with her, with the avowed intention of obtaining easy access to India. When the British Governor-General of India has ascertained that the then Amir, Dost Muhammad Khan, had received assistance in money from Russia, and was endeavouring to gain over the rulers of Sind in the conflict about Herat, which had been invaded by the Persians, he, on October 1st, 1838, declared war.

In justice, however, to Dost Muhammad it must be said that he made every effort to remain on terms of friendship with us, and in this he was ably supported by Sir Alexander Burnes, our agent at that time in Kabul. But Lord Auckland (the Governor-General) would not have it. His policy was one of all "take" and no "give." He more than once severely censured Burnes, who was loyally endeavouring to carry out a policy of which he himself did not approve, and eventually at the end of April, 1838, Burnes was compelled to leave Kabul with nothing accomplished.

Vickovitch, the Russian Agent, had arrived in Kabul during the last few days of 1837, and Dost Muhammad, immediately on his arrival, had gone to Burnes for his advice, actually offering to turn the Russian out if only he had the promise of sympathy from the British. Burnes, tied down to his instructions, could promise nothing, the consequence being that, in contrast to his frigid reception on first arrival, Vickovitch four months later was honoured by being publicly paraded through the streets of Kabul, he having promised the Dost everything that the latter wanted.

Thus was the *amir* forced by our "do-nothing" policy, as Burnes termed it, into the Russo-Persian alliance. He saw ere long how specious were the promises of his new friends, who were unable really to assist him. A subaltern of the British Army, Eldred Pottinger, within the walls of Herat, was setting them at defiance.

As an instance of Russians methods, it may here be mentioned what befell the unfortunate Vickovitch. When he returned to Persia in 1839, giving a full account of his mission to the minister at Tehran he was instructed to proceed direct to St. Petersburg. On his arrival there, full of hope—for he had discharged the duty entrusted to him with admirable address—he reported himself, after the customary formality, to Count Nesselrode; but the minister refused to see him. Instead of a flattering welcome, the unhappy envoy was received with a crushing message to the effect that Count Nesselrode "knew no Captain Vickovitch". Vickovitch understood at once the sinister meaning of this message. He knew the character of his government; he was aware of the recent expostulations of Great Britain, and he saw clearly that he was to be sacrificed. He went back to his hotel, wrote a few bitter, reproachful words, burnt all his other papers, and blew out his brains.

Not until the siege of Herat by the Persians had lasted nine months did Lord Auckland, at the eleventh hour, make a demonstration in the Persian Gulf. A battalion of marines and several native regiments were sent from Bombay and landed on the Island of Karrak about the middle of June, 1838. This movement, small though it was, had the most surprising effect, for when the Shah of Persia learnt that unless he withdrew from before Herat it meant war with England, he raised the siege and set out homeward.

The influence of England, greatly impaired by the parsimonious system of late years, was now restored—in a large measure owing to Eldred Pottinger. Nothing was wanting but a conciliatory and liberal policy to secure the Afghan chiefs, now violently roused against Russia by the onslaught on Herat, in the English alliance.

Not only were these favourable circumstances not turned to account, but they were rather rendered a prolific source of evil by the policy of the British Government. Instead of entering into an alliance with Dost Muhammad, the ruler of the people's choice, and who by his vigour and capacity had won for himself a throne by showing he was worthy of it, they determined on dethroning that chief and placing the exiled, dis-crowned sovereign, Shah Shujah, on the throne. The fact of his having proved incapable of ruling or maintaining himself in power and of his having been for thirty years an exile in British India, was considered of less importance than that of having a Sovereign on the throne, who owed his restoration to British interference, and was identified with our government by present interest and past obligation.

Without going into detail, it may at once be said that the result proved that a greater and more lamentable mistake never was committed by any government, It was to the last degree inexpedient for our Indian Empire, for instead of erecting a powerful barrier against the threatening dangers of Russian aggression, it was calculated to weaken that which did already exist, to involve the English Government in the endless maze of Afghan politics, and, instead of bringing to their support a powerful and brave ally, to encumber them by the defence of a distant dependent.

These and other considerations, which were strongly urged upon Lord Auckland by Burnes and those best versed in Afghan affairs, were entirely disregarded by him.

After a brief negotiation with the "Pensioner of Ludhiana," as Shah Shujah was called, a tripartite treaty was concluded at Lahore on June 26th, 1838, between the Governor-General, Ranjit Singh, and Shah Shujah, which, to the infinite astonishment of the latter, restored him to his throne.

The principal articles of the Treaty were:—

That the British Government and the Chiefs of Lahore recognised Shah Shujah as the Sovereign of Afghanistan, and he on his part engaged to cede Peshawar, Attock, and their dependencies to the Rajah of Lahore, the latter undertaking to despatch a body of troops to aid in re-establishing the Afghan prince on the throne;

That the three contracting powers engaged mutually to defend each other in case of attack;

That the *Shah* promised not to enter into any negotiations with any foreign State without the knowledge and consent of the British and Sikh Governments, and bound himself to oppose any power invading the British and Sikh territories;

Lastly, that Shah Shujah promised not to disturb his nephew, the Ruler of Herat, and renounced all claim of supremacy over the Amirs of Sind.

It was at first intended to assist Shah Shujah by only a small British auxiliary force, and the governor-general issued accordingly a proclamation that the *Shah* should enter Afghanistan surrounded by his own troops.

With this view, 4,000 Irregulars were raised and placed under the nominal command of Prince Timur, his eldest son, but really directed by Captain Wade and other British officers, and paid entirely by the British Treasury.

To this force were to be added 6,000 Sikhs, under Ranjit Singh's generals, and the Sikh Rajah was also to station a force of 15,000 men in observation about Peshawar.

It soon transpired, however, that such troops would not suffice, and that if Shah Shujah was really to be restored it must be accomplished by a British force capable of overrunning Afghanistan.

The British force destined for the expedition was known by the somewhat high-sounding title of "The Army of the Indus," after the style of Napoleon's bulletins, and was all assembled at Ferozpore towards the latter part of November, 1838. It amounted to some 28,000 men (including but one British cavalry regiment and three British infantry battalions), with 100,000 followers and 60,000 transport animals.

The Command-in-Chief was vested in General Sir Henry Fane, the then Commander-in-Chief in India, in whom the troops had unbounded confidence.

The Sikh forces had also concentrated in the vicinity, and before any move forward was made, a series of magnificent reviews and pageants by both armies took place, lasting until the extreme end of November.

News had by this time arrived of the raising of the siege of Herat and the retreat of the Persian Army. This did not deter Lord Auckland from despatching the expedition, determined as he now was to depose Dost Muhammad,; but less preparation was now deemed necessary, and a part only of the assembled force received orders to move forward.

It consisted of:—

Three brigades of infantry.
One strong brigade of cavalry.
A considerable number of siege, horse, and field guns, amounting to some 9,500 men of all arms, termed "The Bengal Army," while 6,000 more were raised as Shah Shujah's contingent.

Sir Henry Fane, on the reduction of the force, resigned the command, which passed to Sir John Keane, another Peninsula veteran, but one who was not so well known to the troops. He was at that time in command of the Bombay Army, then moving from that port by sea to Karachi, and would assume the Command-in-Chief of the expedition on the junction of the two divisions. Meanwhile Sir Willoughby Cotton commanded the Bengal, Army.

Shah Shujah's contingent, under Major-General Simpson, passed through Ferozpore on December 2nd, 1838, and the Bengal Army followed on the 10th.

The route chosen ran S.W. through Bahawalpore to Bukkur, where the Indus was crossed and a north-westerly course was pursued, passing through Shikarpore, Dadur, Quetta, and the Khojak, to Kandahar. The devious route thus adopted was rendered unavoidable, as Ranjit Singh did not wish the force to pass through the Punjab, and, in addition, the Amirs of Sind had to be coerced.

The Bengal Army, moving parallel to the Sutlej, availed themselves of water-carriage, and their sick, hospital stores, and some of the supplies were sent on in boats, which were subsequently to be used in bridging the Indus.

Bahawalpore was reached on December 29th, Sind territory entered near Subzulkote on January 14th, 1839, and the Fort of Bukkur occupied on January 29th.

The enormous number of 30,000 camels and 38,000 camp followers accompanied the Bengal Army, only 9,500 fighting men strong.

Kaye comments thus on this:—

Sir Henry Fane had exhorted the officers of the Army of the Indus not to encumber themselves with large establishments and unnecessary equipages; but there is a natural disposition on the part of Englishmen in all quarters of the globe to carry their comforts, with them. It requires a vast deal of exhortation to induce officers to move lightly equipped. The more difficult the country into which they are sent—the more barbarous the inhabitants—the more trying the climate, the greater is their anxiety to surround themselves with the comforts which remote countries and uncivilised people cannot supply, and which ungenial climates render more indispensable.

It is on record that one officer of the 16th Lancers took with him forty servants!

The Amirs of Sind now proved somewhat refractory with regard to a war contribution levied on them, and so Cotton and Keane (who had now arrived by sea) were despatched on either bank of the Indus against Hyderabad, the capital of Sind. The two columns were entirely ignorant of each other's operations, and so thus early was the want of a proper intelligence department painfully apparent.

Shah Shujah with his contingent was now at Shikarpore, and he was there joined by Macnaghten, who had been appointed political director of the campaign. The latter looked on this movement on Hyderabad as converting the expedition for the restoration of Shah Shujah into a campaign in Sind, and arrested it. Thus began the friction between the military and political authorities, which was hereafter, as will be seen, in constant evidence.

Cotton retraced his steps to Rohri, crossed the Indus, and reached Shikarpore on February 20th.

While the *Shah* remained halted there with his contingent, Cotton resumed his advance on the 23rd, reaching Dadur at the mouth of the Bolan Pass, a distance of 146 miles, on March 10th. These sixteen marches were only accomplished with great difficulty, water and forage being so scarce as to entail great privations on the animals, large numbers of them dying. Cotton now had a month's supplies on his transport animals, and seeing little or no chance of collecting more, he resumed his march on the 16th, entering the Bolan.

The pass is nearly 60 miles in length, and its passage was accomplished in six days. Burnes had gone on in advance and obtained the aid of the Baluchi authorities, and though in consequence the difficulties remaining were only physical, these were far from being inconsiderable.

On March 26th, Quetta was reached. It is described as "a most miserable, mud town, with. a castle on a mound, on which was a small gun on a rickety carriage"; and here again the prospect of raising supplies seemed hopeless.

Sir Willoughby Cotton acted promptly. He sent his adjutant-general back for orders, and Burnes was despatched to Kelat, where he was successful to a certain degree in raising some supplies. The troops were meanwhile placed on reduced rations.

The *Shah* and his contingent moved from Shikarpore on March 7th, followed by Sir John Keane and the Bombay Division. Headquarters were eventually established at Quetta on April 6th, and Keane assumed the supreme command.

31

The march was resumed next day, one brigade, under General Nott, being left to garrison Quetta. No resistance was offered during the passage of the Khojak, and the *Shah* and his contingent now headed the force, being joined by many chiefs and people of the neighbourhood.

Macnaghten obtained authentic information of the flight of the Kandahar *sirdars* towards Persia, and on April 25th Shah Shujah entered the chief city of Western Afghanistan, accompanied by the British envoy, his staff, and the principal officers of his contingent. The wearied troops now found rest and food. Their privations on the march, entirely unopposed though it was, had been enormous; 20,000 animals had perished, and their remains had for a considerable time been the principal food of the men, whose rations had been reduced to one quarter the normal quantity; while of water, so great had been the lack throughout, that historians relate that at times there was not even enough to mix the medicines of the sick.

The brief local excitement which greeted Shah Shujah on his entry into Kandahar was by no means national enthusiasm. When the first outbreak of curiosity had subsided the feeling which remained was one of sullen indifference. Murmurs were heard against the *infidels*, and it was soon apparent that his throne could only be obtained by British bayonets.

Meanwhile the Army of the Indus remained inactive at Kandahar. Supplies had to be collected, and in order to obtain them in sufficient quantities, it was necessary to await the ripening of the crops.

On May 9th a brigade was despatched, under Colonel Sale, to Ghirishk, 75 miles west, in pursuit of the fugitive *sirdars*, but no resistance was encountered, they having fled across the Persian border. Sale accordingly returned to Kandahar.

Eventually the army resumed its march on June 27th, by which time the harvest had ripened, and the transport animals gained strength, but sickness was very prevalent among the troops, and money was becoming scarce. On July 21st the army was before the fortress of Ghazni, situated 230 miles from Kandahar, and 90 miles from Kabul.

Dost Muhammad had thought for some time that the British intended to march from Kandahar on Herat. He now saw that in this he was at fault, and believed that they were advancing direct on Kabul, merely masking Ghazni, *en route.*

Of his three sons, Akbar Khan was opposing the advance of the Shahzada Timur through the Khyber; Hyder Khan was in command of the garrison of Ghazni; and Afzul Khan, with a body of horsemen, was in the vicinity of that place, with instructions to operate on the flanks of the British in the open.

The Afghans had long boasted of the strength of Ghazni, and believed that it could not be taken by assault. On the other hand, Sir John Keane, in spite of the fact that a battering train had been brought to Kandahar by dint of great labour, and at great expense, and although he knew that he was approaching the strongest fortress in the country, known to be garrisoned by the enemy, and certain to be vigorously, defended, still insisted on leaving his heavy guns at Kandahar, and advanced upon Ghazni with nothing but light field pieces, quite unequal to breaching; the walls.

The town itself was insignificant, but the strength of the citadel—deemed impregnable throughout Asia—and its position, commanding the road from Kandahar to Kabul, made it a post of the highest military importance.

The rampart of masonry, sixty feet high, was built on a scarped mount, thirty-five feet high, rising from a wet ditch and defended by numerous towers and skilfully constructed outworks.

To illustrate its size, it may be mentioned that within the citadel there was stabling sufficient for an entire brigade of cavalry.

Hyder Khan had walled up all the gates to prevent them being blown in, except the one on the Kabul side.

Dost Muhammad, never dreaming that the British would attempt to take the place by a "*coup de main,*" thought they would mask it, and took up a strong position himself twenty miles from Kabul, intending, that, while he engaged them in front, Hyder Khan, with part of his garrison, and Afzul Khan, with his horsemen, should fall on their rear and flanks.

His plan was foiled, for one of his own nephews, Abdul Reshed Khan, had deserted from the garrison and revealed to the chief engineer of the force, the weak point, where an assault might be hazarded, namely, the Kabul Gate.

Accordingly, on July 22nd, a storming party, consisting of the light companies of the four European regiments, under Colonel Dennie, of the 13th Light Infantry, was formed, while the main supporting column was composed of the other companies of these regiments under Brigadier Sale.

The night was dark and gusty, and while the storming party and supports were forming up on the Kabul road, the attention of the defenders was attracted to the Kandahar side by heavy fire, kept up at random by the guns.

At 3 a.m. all was ready for the assault. The Afghans were now revealing themselves on the Kandahar side, ready to resist the anticipated attack from that quarter, by a row of blue lights. The stormers having meanwhile silently piled their powder-bags against the Kabul Gate, quite unobserved, Lieutenant Durand successfully exploded the charge. A column of black smoke was seen to rise, and huge masses of masonry and beams, lifted up by the force of the explosion, came down with a tremendous crash. Colonel Dennie, heading the stormers, gained the opening before the defenders could reach it. A desperate struggle then took place, the British gradually gaining ground.

Sale, pressing forward in support, met an engineer officer, who, thrown to the ground and bewildered by the explosion, reported that the opening was blocked by the ruins, and that Dennie was unable to force an entry. Sale at first halted, uncertain what to do, and then began to retreat, but very soon Dennie's bugler was heard sounding "the advance," and back went the column. The Afghans had not failed to profit by the respite thus afforded them, and showed a resolute front at the gateway. A hand-to-hand fight took place, in which the brigadier himself was cut down, but regaining his feet, he led his column into the fortress, and, other troops coming up, the capture of Ghazni was complete, and the British colours planted on the ramparts.

There was still some hard fighting within the walls, but those who ceased to resist were spared, and the women respected. Hyder Khan was immediately afterwards captured with 1,600 other prisoners, fed vast stores of ammunition, guns, and provisions fell into the hands of the victors, whose loss were 17 killed and 165 wounded, 18 of these were officers. 500 Afghans were buried, besides a great number who fell in the cavalry pursuit.

The fall of Ghazni was a mortal stroke to Dost Muhammad. Afzul Khan, approaching on the 22nd, prepared to fall on the "beaten invaders," was so astounded and terror struck at the sight of the British Colours waving on the citadel, that he at once abandoned his baggage, elephants, and camp stores, all of which were appropriated by the British, and fled forthwith towards Kabul.

In vain Dost Muhammad endeavoured to get his army to give battle; his men, in response to his appeals, deserted to the victors: it was the counterpart of Napoleon at Fontainebleau. He had perforce on August 2nd to turn back, forsaken by all but a small band, and ride through Kabul to the far side of the Bamian, whither a small band of horsemen pursued him ineffectually for a few days.

Next day, the 3rd, the news of his flight reached the British, who had moved forward from Ghazni on July 30th. Dost Muhammad's guns, 22 in number, were found in position abandoned *en route*, and Kabul was reached on 7th August. Again, no enthusiasm was evinced by the populace at the reoccupation of the Bala Hissar (the citadel) by Shah Shujah after an exile of thirty years.

The object of the expedition was apparently attained, and the *Shah* restored to what was fondly hoped to be an undisputed throne. Satisfaction was almost universal in England, and only a few, among whom was the Duke of Wellington, maintained that our difficulties were now only about commence and that the lesson of Moscow in 1812 should be borne in mind.

The operations of Wade's force by way of the Khyber were dwarfed by the more ostentatious ones of Sir John Keane; but it was in no small measure owing to these operations that the resistance to the main army was so slight. For a long time, Dost Muhammad regarded the movement through the Khyber more anxiously than that of the Army of the Indus. Akbar Khan never met Wade in the field, but his force was drawn away from the decisive point at a time when it might have been of great use in the west, and it is in no small measure owing to this division of the *amir's* military strength that he was unable to offer any effectual resistance to the British advance from Kandahar.

Wade reached Kabul on September 3rd, and brought Sir John Keane's force up to a total of 15,000 men.

It was still patent that, were the British force withdrawn, Shah Shujah would be deposed, Dost Muhammad reinstated, and that the latter, from motives of revenge, would undoubtedly ally himself with Russia. Thus, not only would all objects of the expedition be lost, but the very danger it was undertaken to avert would be enhanced.

Lord Auckland decided to withdraw the major portion of the Bombay Army by way of the Bolan, and most of the cavalry and horse artillery of the Bengal Army, under Sir John Keane, *via* the Khyber, leaving troops at Jellalabad, Kabul, Ghazni, and Kandahar, besides a small detachment near the Bamian Pass to watch Dost Muhammad: the whole under the command of Sir Willoughby Cotton.

The Bombay Army started on its homeward march on September 18th, taking Kelat *en route,* on November 13th, with a loss of 32 killed and 107 wounded. Keane and his force left Kabul on October 2nd.

Afghanistan was now governed by a trinity, practically co-equal:—

Shah Shujah, the nominal ruler;
Macnaghten, the political agent; and
Cotton, the military commander;

and the evils of this system were soon felt. The various detachments did not meet with any overt opposition; but they soon discovered that most of the clans only wanted a leader and some prospect of success to break out into insurrection.

To add to this, news came to hand from Pottinger at Herat to the effect that Russia, desiring to re-assert her lost prestige in Central Asia, which had been impaired by her failure at Herat the previous year and by the progress of the British in Afghanistan, was sending a force of 6,000 men with 12 guns against Khiva. All through the winter of 1839-1840 this afforded a subject of much anxious thought, and it was not until March 13th, 1840, that it was publicly announced by the St, Petersburg newspapers what a lamentable failure this expedition had been.

It now came to light that the double-faced Vizier of Herat, Yar Muhammad, while living on British bounty, was deep in intrigue with Persia.

In the Punjab Ranjit Singh had died, and the Sikh chiefs, without his loyal guiding spirit, were by no means so well disposed towards us.

The Ghilzaies were in open arms, and had cut the communication between Kabul and Kandahar. A detachment of all arms had to be sent against them, and a defeat of 2,000 on May 16th temporarily suppressed the insurrection in that quarter.

Quetta was meanwhile besieged, and Kelat retaken by the Baluchis on June 28th.

Added to all this, Dost Muhammad, after narrowly escaping with his life from the treacherous Khan of Bokhara, had collected a following of 6,000 Usbegs, and was advancing towards the Bamian. The Gurkha Regiment, holding two posts beyond the pass, was in an unenviable position, for the entire surrounding population was hostile, and a locally raised Afghan regiment had deserted bodily to the enemy. The Gurkhas were accordingly ordered to fall back to the Bamian.

The flame of revolt had now spread throughout the country, but an unexpected check to Dost Muhammad postponed the eventual catastrophe for a year.

On September 18th he advanced down the valley of Bamian,

where he was met by two companies of *sepoys*, two of Gurkhas, two guns, and 400 Afghan Horse, the whole under Lieutenant Murray Mackenzie.

In spite of the great disparity of numbers, the odds being one to five, Mackenzie attacked. The Usbegs at first firmly stood their ground, but the guns coming up to closer range played on them with great effect, and they broke and fled, hotly pursued by the cavalry. The superiority of European arms and discipline was never more clearly proved than on this occasion.

Defeated on the Hindu Kush, Dost Muhammad reappeared in Kohistan. A force under Sir Robert Sale was sent to deal with him, and took two of his fortified posts on September 29th and October 23rd respectively, the first without much difficulty, but the second only after hard fighting and a repulse. On November 2nd Dost Muhammad gained a success over Sale at Parwandarrah, only fifty miles from the capital.

Two days afterwards he suddenly appeared at Kabul, unattended and alone, and surrendered himself to Sir William Macnaghten!

It appeared that after the storming of Ghazni and his defeat in the Bamian he had despaired of his cause, and had only been waiting for a success before giving himself up, in order to be able to do so with untarnished personal honour. On November 12th he was sent under strong escort to India.

The Afghan combination was now deprived of its most formidable character—unity of direction. This fact and two events which synchronised with Dost Muhammad's voluntary surrender contributed in a material degree temporarily to tranquilise the country. On November 3rd General Nott reoccupied Kelat, and on December 1st Colonel Marshall totally defeated a large body of insurgents under the son of the ex-chief of that fortress at Kotri, with a loss to them of 500 men, together with all their guns and baggage.

At the end of the year 1840 there was a renewed insurrection in the neighbourhood of Kandahar. The political direction of this province was now in the hands of Major (afterwards Sir Henry) Rawlinson of the Native Army, and the military under General Nott. The latter despatched a detachment of cavalry and guns to quell the disturbance under Captain Farrington, who came upon 1,500 of the rebel horse on January 3rd, 1841, and inflicted on them a severe defeat. Thus, for a time the soldier had done his work. The more difficult task of the politician was to seek for the causes of dissatisfaction and recommend the means for putting down the spirit of revolt. Rawlinson did his work most thoroughly, but unfortunately his views did not commend themselves to the ever-optimistic Macnaghten, and his warnings were disregarded.

Affairs in Herat had been steadily working up to a crisis, and on February 8th Yar Muhammad, the *vizier*, when deep in intrigue with Persia against us, formulated a series of preposterous demands to Major Todd, our political agent. These the latter had no alternative but to refuse, which done, he turned his back on the place.

Nothing of much moment now occurred until early in May, 1841, when the Ghilzaies appeared in force near the fort of Khelat-i-Ghilzaie on the Kabul-Kandahar road, which we had commenced rebuilding preparatory to stationing in it a strong garrison to act as a curb to the adjacent tribes. Against this they forcibly protested.

Nott sent Colonel Wymer, with a mixed column about 1,200 strong with four guns, to dislodge a somewhat formidable gathering of 5,000 tribesmen. Wymer was compelled to act on the defensive, as he had a large convoy to protect. The Ghilzaies came on in three columns, attacking in front and on both flanks. The native infantry received them again and again with steady musketry fire, and the guns co-operating effectively, after a struggle of five hours the Ghilzaies gave way, having suffered heavily.

The proceedings of the Duranis, the royal clan, gave equal cause for alarm. Under a chief by name Akbar Khan, a body of 3,000 was under arms before Ghirishk, and even Macnaghten realised that it was essential to strike a blow.

Under Captain Woodburn, commanding one of the *Shah's* regiments, a column of 900 infantry, two guns, and a small body of Afghan horse, set out, and on July 3rd found the enemy posted on the far side of the Helmand, now 6,000 strong and mustered in six divisions with a *mullah* at the head of each. Woodburn tried the fords, but found none passable. This was in the early morning; at 4 p.m. the enemy commenced the passage of the river at previously known points. They made a spirited advance, but the infantry, well supported by the guns, repulsed every attack, and before daybreak the Duranis withdrew.

Unfortunately, the success could not be followed up, as no reliance could be placed in the Afghan horse. Woodburn pushed on to Ghirishk, and warned Macnaghten of the disturbed state of the country. Rawlinson from Kandahar again wrote; in a similar strain, but the warnings were once more unheeded and denounced as idle statements by the infatuated envoy, who censured his correspondents for what he called their "unwarrantably gloomy views."

In corroboration of Rawlinson, Akbar Khan soon appeared again at the head of the insurrection in Western Afghanistan, and a force of 350 *sepoys*, 800 horse, and four guns, under Captain Griffin, who had been sent to reinforce Woodburn, was despatched early in August against the rebel chief. On August 17th he was encountered, strongly posted with 3,500 men in a succession of walled gardens and mud forts, from which a heavy fire was maintained against the assailants. The attack with good combination of guns and infantry was successful, and this time the cavalry, headed by the young Prince Saftar Jang, a son of Shah Shujah, charged with great effect, and the Duranis were defeated and dispersed with great slaughter. The Ghilzaies, too, had received another check, Colonel Chambers, with a detachment of 1,500 men, having scattered a large body of them on August 5th.

These repeated successes were followed by a lull, and had the disastrous effect of inspiring false confidence in the authorities at Kabul, Sir Willoughby Cotton had been succeeded by General Elphinstone, a veteran of the Wellington school, who had commanded a regiment at Waterloo, He is described by Kaye as:

> A man of high connections, aristocratic influence, and agreeable manners, but entirely unacquainted with Eastern warfare; a martyr to the gout, which rendered him utterly unfit for personal activity, or even sometimes to sit on horseback, and, as the event proved, though personally brave, possessed of none of the mental energy or forethought which might supply its place.

How he should have been selected for this arduous situation, when these disqualifications were common knowledge, and when such men as Pollock, Nott, and Sale were on the spot, is one of the mysteries of official conduct never likely to be cleared up, for everyone subsequently shunned the responsibility of his appointment.

The force actually in and about Kabul now consisted of one European, two *sepoy*, and two Afghan infantry regiments, a regiment of native cavalry, one troop of foot and one of horse artillery, and a train of mountain guns—5,000 fighting men in all, encumbered by exactly three times this number of camp followers.

Had this force been judiciously posted and properly directed, it was perfectly adequate to deal with any troops that the Afghans could have brought against it, for besides the possession of a train of artillery with ample ammunition they had the Bala Hissar, an immensely strong citadel, situated on a steep height and commanding every part of the city. But, *Quos Deus vult perdere prius dementat*, and all these advantages were voluntarily thrown away; the troops were placed in a low cantonment outside both the citadel and the walls, commanded on all sides by heights and buildings, having been withdrawn from the Bala Hissar by Macnaghten's orders to make way for 160 ladies of the *harem*! To crown all, the commissariat stores for the whole winter were separate again from the cantonment, with which they were connected by an undefended passage, commanded by the King's Garden, a walled enclosure, and Muhammad Sharif's Fort.

The responsibility for these measures rested entirely with Sir William Macnaghten, who sacrificed everything to a show of security. Still blind to the reiterated warnings of Burnes and Rawlinson, he persisted in writing of everything as *couleur de rose*. He had just been appointed Governor of Bombay, and was on the eve of handing to Burnes and leaving for India, when at last the inevitable storm brewing for so long burst on November 2nd with the utmost violence.

One of the first attacks was made on the house of the unfortunate Burnes, who, though warned of the danger, refused to leave his post, the consequence being that he, with his brother, servants, and guard were murdered to a man. The Treasury was next assailed, the guard of 28 *sepoys* and every human being there massacred, and loot to the amount of 7,000 sterling carried off. The mob, now greatly increased, proceeded to loot, burn, and massacre indiscriminately in all parts of the city.

While these events were taking place, 5,000 British troops remained inactive in their cantonments within half-an-hour's march, and not a man was ordered out! Had the least attempt at reprisal been carried out before the mob grew in size, the Afghans themselves subsequently admitted that the insurrection must have been quashed.

Later in the day, Brigadier Shelton's brigade and four guns were moved into the Bala Hissar, but all the remaining troops were kept where they were. Shelton recommended prompt and decisive measures, but was over-ruled by Macnaghten and Elphinstone, and with them rested equally the responsibility of supineness and inactivity.

Next day the detachment from Khurd Kabul, two miles east, was recalled, and succeeded in reaching the cantonments.

The only effort against the insurgents was made by three companies and two horse artillery guns. So weak a detachment against an enemy now swelled to thousands and excited by the *mullahs* to a high pitch of fanaticism, was foredoomed to failure. Fortunately, it retired in good time.

The next disaster was the seizure of the little detached commissariat fort with all its stories on November 4th, Ensign Warren, in command of its garrison of 80 men, sent repeated messages for help, but obtained none, and at last, recognising that resistance there was futile, fought his way to the cantonment.

The same day a similar and scarcely less serious catastrophe occurred. Macnaghten had insisted some time previously on the removal of about 600 tons of ground wheat from the Bala Hissar to some camel sheds on the outskirts of the city: here Captain Colin Mackenzie, commanding the small guard, was attacked on November 2nd, and after holding out for two days, was compelled to adopt a similar course to that of Warren. The enemy then proceeded to occupy the remaining forts round the cantonment.

It was now evident to every man on both sides that it was out of the question for the British to maintain themselves in the capital throughout the winter, for they had lost all their supplies, and it was impossible, with the ground under snow and with every village in the hands of the Afghans, to attempt to collect enough to last them; moreover, even could reinforcements from India force their way to Kabul at that time of year, they would only add to the number of mouths to be fed.

Nothing was done for two days, during which time the Afghans were permitted to carry away supplies looted from us, within 400 yards of the cantonment.

At length, on 6th November, in response to the unanimous clamour of the men, a storming party carried an outlying fort, and various minor, but decisive, successes were gained, showing that had the troops been properly directed, and a general battle brought on, the enemy undoubtedly would have been defeated.

The commissariat officers, too, had shown enterprise, and had procured some supplies from neighbouring villages on payment, so that, the troops being placed on half rations, the pressing difficulty of subsistence had been surmounted.

General Elphinstone now became alarmed about ammunition, although there was a full two months' supply, and, refusing to listen to any active measures, counselled only a capitulation. His health had become so bad that Brigadier Shelton was sent out from the citadel to help him. Elphinstone's jealousy, however, thwarted him, orders were given and countermanded, plans discussed and their decision deferred, and it soon transpired that, from the disunion of their chiefs, the troops were in a more parlous plight than ever.

The Rikabashi Fort, situated at the north-east angle of the cantonment, was taken with some difficulty on November 10th, Elphinstone refusing to allow our cavalry to co-operate, in spite of the troops being twice charged in flank by the Afghan Horse, who nearly turned the day in their favour. This success afforded a further breathing space to the commissariat officers, who again turned it to good account.

On November 13th there was an action on the Bemaru Heights, north-west of the cantonment, where the enemy had appeared in force and fired with two guns into the cantonment itself. Brigadier Shelton was sent out with four squadrons of cavalry, two guns, and sixteen companies to dislodge them. After some trouble the enemy were driven away and the guns taken, and one, a four-pounder, brought in; but the other was spiked and abandoned.

This was the last success achieved, and nothing but a list of blunders and disasters remains to be recorded.

The enemy remained quiet for some days, and urgent messages were sent by Macnaghten to McGregor and Rawlinson, the political agents at Jellalabad and Kandahar, to send their whole disposable forces.

The requisitions placed the officers in a great dilemma; the envoy's orders, ought to be obeyed and the very existence of the troops in the capital might depend on instant relief being afforded, while, on the other hand, affairs in Kabul were so desperate from the scarcity of, supplies, that any additional mouths would court certain destruction of the whole.

After great deliberation McGregor and Sale resolved to disobey the order, and keep their troops at Jellalabad, and although Rawlinson: and Nott despatched a force from Kandahar, the draught cattle perished so rapidly, that, after a few days, it was forced to retrace its steps.

A further calamity now befell the British in the total annihilation of the Gurkha Regiment in Kohistan, on November 13th, after a most gallant stand against overwhelming odds, the sole survivors being one officer, one Gurkha, and Eldred Pottinger, who reached Kabul half-dead with wounds.

The only practical course now open was to move every man available with all the provisions that could be obtained into the Bala Hissar:

this, was favoured by Shah Shujah, while the engineers had counselled it from the first.

It is interesting to note that in Lord Stanhope's book, *Conversations with the Duke of Wellington*, the duke is recorded to have; observed that the opinion he had formed on reading all accounts, was, that:

> If on the day after Burnes' murder, the troops had occupied the Bala Hissar and removed thither all their stores, they would have been perfectly secure, but that three weeks later, if even an angel had come down from Heaven, he could not then have saved them.

Elphinstone had no opinion to offer on the subject of the move, and Macnaghten, unfortunately, yielded to. Shelton's vehement arguments against such a course, as being, in his opinion, dangerous and discreditable.

Akbar Khan, Dost Muhammad's son, and the force which had cut up the Gurkhas in Kohistan, arrived at this juncture to augment the Afghan numbers.

Correspondence with a view to capitulation was opened, but before terms could be agreed upon a most disastrous action was fought, which hastened the crisis.

For the first three weeks of November, in spite of the blockade, the commissaries had managed to obtain a certain quantity of grain, chiefly from the village of Bemaru; the Afghans determined to close this source of supply, and posted troops accordingly.

Macnaghten urged an immediate attack, and a feeble attempt was made on November 22nd, but the enterprise miscarried.

Next day the attack was renewed with five companies of British and twelve of native infantry, three squadrons of native cavalry, 100 sappers, and a single Horse Artillery gun. (Why one gun only was taken when there plenty available does not transpire.) Swarms of Afghans from the city swelled the numbers of the enemy, and Shelton drew up his 1,400 men in two squares, with the gun in front and the cavalry in rear. The Afghans had the great: advantage that their matchlocks outranged the British muskets, and they used this to the full. Shelton's ammunition ran out, and so demoralised were the troops that when called upon to use their bayonets, not a musket was brought down to the charge, even in the English companies.

The Afghans, in bravado, planted a standard within thirty paces of the British ranks: not a man advanced to take it. The officers did their

LAST STAND AT GANDAMAK

utmost, and for lack of ammunition stood in front and hurled stones at the enemy. A sudden rush captured the gun, which had been well served, but it was soon retaken, the enemy driven back in confusion, and their leader killed.

This was the crisis of the day, and had General Elphinstone acceded to Macnaghten's request to send out reinforcements, all might have been restored. The former, however, gave a flat refusal, saying that it: was a wild scheme.

Fresh swarms of the enemy appeared on the scene, and the British were losing heavily, yet nothing would induce them to close with the Afghans, so thorough was their demoralisation. An unexpected flank attack completed their discomfiture, and a panic seized the whole force; the gunners gallantly endeavoured to save their gun, but failed, every one of them being killed or wounded. All order was lost, and the whole force, led by the British companies, rushed helter-skelter for cantonments. The Afghans failed to follow up their success, or the cantonments themselves must have been taken.

This disastrous defeat, in which we lost 178 killed and 55 wounded, put an end to military operations, and made it imperative to arrange the best terms of capitulation possible.

On December 11th negotiations with the enemy were opened, and on the 13th the Bala Hissar was evacuated under a treaty, which also provided for a safe conduct of the troops to India and for provision of carriage and supplies. Shah Shujah was to return to India, Dost Muhammad to be restored to Kabul, and the Afghans were not to contract any alliance without our consent.

The Afghans made no attempt to keep their part of the agreement, and on December 23rd Macnaghten, on going unescorted to a conference with their chiefs, was treacherously murdered by Akbar Khan, who used a pistol that Macnaghten himself had given him the previous day.

Though the spot where this occurred was not a quarter of a mile from the cantonment, no attempt at rescue or reprisal was made, or, indeed, even considered. The body was left lying on the plain, whence it was finally carried off, hacked to pieces, to the bazaar, there to be exhibited to an applauding multitude. It seems incredible that British troops and British generals could have sunk to such depths of demoralisation and degradation as to remain inactive on such an occasion.

After the murder of Macnaghten, Major Pottinger undertook the political duties of the mission, and met the chiefs in conference. Some fresh conditions were imposed, chief of which was the surrender of all but six of the guns.

On January 6th, 1842, though neither of the terms as to transport or escort had been fulfilled by the Afghan chiefs, the retreat was commenced:

690 European troops;
970 native cavalry; and
2,840 native infantry;
in all, 4,500 fighting men, with 12,000 camp followers besides women and children, left the cantonment.

The horrors of this march have been graphically described by Kaye, Alison, and Lady Sale.

From the time that the rearguard filed out on the 6th, until the 13th, when the last survivors (except Dr. Brydon, who managed to struggle alone to Jellalabad), perished at Gandamak, a continuous fire was kept up by swarms of tribesmen on either flank, added to which intense suffering was caused by cold and snow. The widows, married people, and children were given up to Akbar Khan on the 9th, and General Elphinstone, Brigadier Shelton, and Captain Johnson were forcibly detained after a conference at Jagdalak on the 12th. Elphinstone died in captivity on April 25th; Shah Shujah was murdered on the 5th of that month.

Space does not permit of the recital of Sale's and Nott's gallant defence of Jellalabad and Kandahar respectively, or of Pollock's passage of the Khyber and his subsequent victorious march from Jellalabad on Kabul, which he reached on September 15th, 1842; while Nott advanced on the capital from Kandahar, but in conclusion we may briefly examine the causes of the British disasters, and consider the lessons to be drawn from them.

Firstly: The injustice of overturning the reigning power in an independent State, and the forcing of a hated dynasty on a reluctant people.

For a trifling sum Dost Muhammad, the ruler of the people's choice, was willing to shut his gates against Russia and to enter into the British alliance. Instead of closing with his proposals we decided to dethrone him, and place a king on the throne to be a mere puppet in our hands.

A mistake in policy, and a crime in morality.

Secondly: The errors in the conception of the expedition, which was thrown forward 1,000 miles from its base of operations through a desert and mountainous country, peopled by barbarous and hostile tribes, bring to mind, the Moscow Campaign of 1812; but the Indian Government did not, like Napoleon, endeavour to repair its error by moving up strong bodies to keep up communications with the rear.

Thirdly: The force employed was inadequate and out of proportion to the object in view, and the stiffening of British troops insufficient. Moreover, when British reinforcements were sent, they largely consisted of raw recruits.

It was the old story of England having disbanded a veteran force on a peace being declared, and trusting to making a civilian into a soldier by putting arms into his hands and a uniform on his back. Present-day politicians would do well to lay this lesson to heart.

Fourthly: The lack of harmony, and intimate co-operation between the political and military authorities from start to finish.

This was unfortunately for many years only too common, a feature of Indian Frontier Campaigns.

Fifthly: The extreme errors in the military arrangements; the neglect to occupy and hold the Bala Hissar; the mistake in placing the troops in exposed and ill-fortified cantonments with magazines and commissariat separate again; the want of decision on the part of the general; these and other fatal errors conduced to the demoralisation of the troops, who failed at critical moments as British troops seldom do.

Lastly: The ill-considered appointment by a Whig Cabinet of a man, totally unfitted for command, ignorant of the country, people, and language, when better men, well versed in the local conditions and experienced in the type of warfare, were available on the spot.

CHAPTER 5

The Defeat of the Biluchis: 1842

For a time, affairs in Scinde, after the Afghanistan disasters, looked peaceable; but the conditions proposed by new treaties to the *amirs*, in the infringements upon their game preserves, and the abolition of transit duties, occasioned some discontent. Gradually this jealousy of the Scinde chieftains ripened into hatred; and while evasive policy was resorted to by the *amirs*, a corps, under Sir Charles Napier, advanced to support the British representative, Major Outram.

The agency had been attacked, gallantly defended, and Outram effected an honourable retreat; while the *amirs*, collecting in great force at Fulali, Sir Charles, with his small force, determined to attack them. An extract from his own despatch will best describe this daring and most brilliant affair:—

> On the 16th I marched to Muttaree, having there ascertained that the *amirs* were in position at Miani (ten miles' distance), to the number of 22,000 men, and well knowing that a delay for reinforcements would both strengthen their confidence and add to their numbers, already seven times that which I commanded, I resolved to attack them, and we marched at 4 a.m. on the morning of the 17th; at eight o'clock the advanced guard discovered their camp; at nine o'clock we formed in order of battle, about 2,800 men of all arms, and twelve pieces of artillery. We were now within range of the enemy's guns, and fifteen pieces of artillery opened upon us, and were answered by our cannon. The enemy were very strongly posted, woods were on their flanks, which I did not think could be burned. These two woods were joined by the dry bed of the River Fallali, which had a high bank. The bed of the river was nearly straight, and about 1,200 yards in length. Behind this and in both woods

were the enemy posted. In front of their extreme right, and on the edge of the wood, was a village. Having made the best examination of their position which so short a time permitted, the artillery was posted on the right of the line, and some skirmishers of infantry, with the Scinde Irregular Horse, were sent in front to try and make the enemy show his force more distinctly; we then advanced from the right in echelon of battalions, refusing the left to save it from the fire of the village.

The 9th Bengal Light Cavalry formed the reserve in rear of the left wing; and the Poona Horse, together with four companies of infantry, guarded the baggage. In this order of battle, we advanced as at a review across a fine plain swept by the cannon of the enemy. The artillery and H. M.'s 22nd regiment in line, formed the leading echelon, the 25th N.I. the second, the 12th N.I. the third, and the 1st Grenadier N.I. the fourth.

The enemy was 1,100 yards from our line, which soon traversed the intervening space. Our fire of musketry opened at about 100 yards from the bank in reply to that of the enemy; and in a few minutes the engagement became general along the bank of the river, on which the combatants fought for about three hours or more with great fury, man to man. Then was seen the superiority of the musket and bayonet over the sword and shield and matchlock. The brave Biluchis first discharging their matchlocks and pistols, dashed over the bark with desperate resolution; but down went these bold and skilful swordsmen under the superior power of the musket and bayonet. At one time the courage and numbers of the enemy against the 22nd, the 25th, and the 12th regiments bore heavily in that part of the battle.

There was no time to be lost, and I sent orders to the cavalry to force the right of the enemy's line. This order was very gallantly executed by the 9th Bengal cavalry and the Scinde Horse; the struggle on our right and centre was at that moment so fierce that I could not go to the left. In this charge the 9th Light Cavalry took a standard and several pieces of artillery, and the Scinde Horse took the enemy's camp, from which a vast body of their cavalry slowly retired fighting. Lieutenant Fitzgerald gallantly pursued them for two miles, and, I understand, slew three of the enemy in single combat. The brilliant conduct of these two cavalry regiments decided in my opinion the crisis of the action, for from the moment the cavalry were seen in rear

Bolan Pass Balochistan, 1842

of their right flank, the resistance of our opponents slackened; the 22nd regiment forced the bank, the 25th and 12th did the same, the latter regiment capturing several guns, and the victory was decided. The artillery made great havoc among the dense masses of the enemy, and dismounted several of their guns. The whole of the enemy's artillery, ammunition, standards, and camp, with considerable stores and some treasure, were taken.

War was now regularly proclaimed, and on the 22nd of March the Sikhs recommenced hostilities at Mattari, Sir Charles Napier, in the meanwhile, having effected a junction with his reinforcements. Halting at the village of Duppa, on the 23rd, he decided on attacking the Biluchis on the 24th. The enemy were in a strong position, numbering 20,000 men. The Anglo-Indian Army might amount in round numbers to 5,000, all arms included. Thus runs the despatch:—

The forces under my command marched from Hyderabad this morning at daybreak. About half-past 8 o'clock we discovered and attacked the army under the personal command of the Meer Shere Mahomed, consisting of twenty thousand men of all arms, strongly posted behind one of those large *nullahs* by which this country is intersected in all directions. After a combat of about three hours, the enemy was wholly defeated with considerable slaughter, and the loss of all his standards and cannon.

His position was nearly a straight line; the *nullah* was formed by two deep parallel ditches, one 20 feet wide and 8 feet deep, the other 42 feet wide and 17 deep, which had been for a long distance freshly scarped, and a banquet made behind the bank expressly for the occasion.

To ascertain the strength of his line was extremely difficult, as his left did not appear to be satisfactorily denned; but he began by moving to his right when he perceived that the British force outflanked him in that direction. Believing that this movement had drawn him from that part of the *nullah* which had been prepared for defence, I hoped to attack his right with less difficulty, and Major Leslie's troop of horse artillery was ordered to move forward and endeavour to rake the *nullah*. The 9th Light Cavalry and Poona Horse advancing in line, on the left of the artillery, which was supported on the right by Her Majesty's 22nd regiment, the latter being, however, at first considerably retired to admit of the oblique fire of Leslie's troop. The whole of the artillery now opened upon the enemy's position, and the British line advanced in echelons from the left, H.M.'s 22nd regiment leading the attack.

The enemy was now perceived to move from his centre in considerable bodies to his left, apparently retreating, unable to sustain the cross-fire of the British artillery; on seeing which Major Stack, at the head of the 3rd Cavalry, under command of Captain Delamain, and the Sindh Horse, under command of Captain Jacob, made a brilliant charge upon the enemy's left flank, crossing the *nullah* and cutting down the retreating enemy for several miles.

While this was passing on the right, H.M.'s 22nd regiment, gallantly led by Major Poole, who commanded the brigade, and Captain George, who commanded the corps, attacked the *nullah* on the left with great gallantry, and I regret to add, with considerable loss. This brave battalion marched up to the *nullah* under a heavy fire of matchlocks, without returning a shot till within forty paces of the entrenchment, and then stormed it like British soldiers. The intrepid Lieutenant Coote first mounted the rampart, seized one of the enemy's standards, and was severely wounded while waving it and cheering on his men.

Meanwhile the Poona Horse, under Captain Tait, and the 9th Cavalry, under Major Story, turned the enemy's right flank pursuing and cutting down the fugitives for several miles. H.M.'s 22nd regiment was well supported by the batteries commanded by Captains Willoughby and Hutt, which crossed their fire with that of Major Leslie. Then came the 2nd brigade under command of Major Woodburn, bearing down into action with excellent coolness. It consisted of the 25th, 21st, and 12th regiments, under the command of Captains Jackson, Stevens, and Fisher, respectively; these regiments were strongly sustained by the fire of Captain Whitley's battery, on the right of which were the 8th and 1st regiments, under Majors Browne and Clibborne; these two corps advanced with the regularity of a review up to the entrenchments, their commanders, with considerable exertion, stopping their fire, on seeing that a portion of the Sindh Horse and 3rd Cavalry in charging the enemy had got in front of the brigade.

The battle was decided by the troop of horse artillery and H.M.'s 22nd regiment.

Battle of Miani, 17th Feb., 1843

CHAPTER 6

The Battle of Moodkee: 1845

The fatal *dénouement* of the retreat from Cabul was still in vivid colouring before the British public, when tidings from the East, announced that it might be considered only as the forerunner of still more alarming demonstrations, and these from a power, fully as unfriendly, and far more formidable to British interests than the Ghiljies and fanatic tribes of Afghanistan. The Punjaub for years had been internally convulsed. The *musnud* in turn was occupied by women whose debaucheries were disgusting, and men who had reached it by the foulest murders. The country was frightfully disorganised; one bond of union alone existed among the Sikhs, and that was the most deadly hostility to the British.

The region of North-Western India, known in modern times under the name of the Punjaub, is remarkably well denned by geographical limits. On the north, it is bounded by one of the Himalaya ranges. On the west by the Khybur and Soliman mountains and the Indus. On the south, and east, the Sutlej divides it from British India. Its area is computed to enclose 85,000 square miles. The arteries of the Indus, namely the Jelum, Chenab, Ravi, Beas, and Sutlej, traverse the whole country, and form its local divisions into what are termed *doabs*. The Punjaub, being translated, hence means "the country of five rivers."

The state of things beyond the Sutlej alarmed the Indian government, and Lord Ellenborough acted with energy and good judgment; Scinde and Gwalior must be deprived of the power of being mischievous, and while the former was annexed in form to the possessions of the Company, Gwalior was being prepared for undergoing a similar change. To give effect to these important measures, an army of observation marched upon the Sutlej, but long before any results from his policy could be developed, Lord Ellenborough was recalled, and Sir Henry Hardinge appointed to succeed him. In the spring of 1844, the new governor reached Calcutta.

The Cabul disasters had rendered the very thought of Eastern war most unpopular at home, and Sir Henry assumed the chief command, with a full determination to avoid a rupture with the Sikhs—could such be avoidable; but that, as events proved, was impossible, and pacific policy was tried and found wanting.

The summer of 1845 was marked by frightful excesses in Lahore. Murder and debauchery went hand-in-hand together; and the *ranee* herself, as well as her chief adviser, Jowar Singh, no longer disguised their purpose of coming to blows with the British. On the part of Jowar Singh, this was but the prosecution of a policy which had long been in favour with him; and as he was heartily detested by the rest of the *sirdars*, they made it a pretext' for conspiring against him and putting him to death. But the *ranee* was swayed by different motives.

From day to day her army became more unmanageable; and she desired, above all things, to get rid of the nuisance, even if her deliverance should come with a victorious British force to Lahore. Accordingly, after having long withstood the clamours of her officers, she gave a hearty, yet a reluctant, consent to the proposed invasion of the protected states; and a plan of operations was drawn up, which indicated no slight knowledge of the art of war on the part of those from whom it emanated.

As yet, Sir Henry had avoided every appearance of angry demonstration. Loodiana and Ferozepore were well garrisoned. The former place was weak—the latter better calculated for resistance. A magazine to supply both places had been judiciously established where the Umballa road touches that of Kurnaul—for Busseean was equally accessible to the garrisons which were threatened.

Coming events had not been disregarded by the chief in command, and in June, Sir Henry in person proceeded to the western provinces. Approaching hostilities had in the autumn become too evident; the Sikhs were advancing to the Sutlej, and instead of having, as formerly reported, 15,000 men in and about Lahore, they had actually seven divisions, which might fairly average, each with the other, 8,000 men. One of these was to remain to garrison the capital, the remainder were disposable, and, as it was believed, destined to attack Loodiana, Kurrachee, Ferozepore, Scinde, and Attock.

Before the subsequent transactions are described, a detail of the strength, organisation, and *matériel* of the Sikh Army, as given at the time by Lieutenant-Colonel Steinbach, formerly in the service of the

THE CHARGE OF THE KING'S OWN LIGHT DRAGOONS AT MUDKI

maharajah, will be interesting:—

This force, consisting of about 110,000 men, is divided into regulars and irregulars; the former of whom, about 70,000 strong, are drilled and appointed according to the European system. The cavalry branch of the disciplined force amounts to nearly 13,000, and the infantry and artillery to 60,000 more. The irregulars, variously armed and equipped, are nearly 40,000 strong, of which number upwards of 20,000 are cavalry, the remainder consisting of infantry and matchlock-men, while the contingents, which the *sirdars* or chiefs are obliged to parade on the requisition of the sovereign, amount to considerably above 30,000 men. The artillery consisted in Runject's time of 376 guns, and 370 swivels mounted on camels or on light carriages adapted to their size. There is no distinct corps of artillery as in other services, but there are 4,000 or 5,000 men, under a *daroga*, trained to the duty of gunners, and these are distributed with the ordnance throughout the regular army.

The costume of the regular infantry is scarlet, with different coloured facings, to distinguish regiments, as in the British service. The trousers are of blue linen; the head-dress is a blue turban, with one end loose, and spread so as to entirely cover the head, back of the neck, and shoulders; the belts are of black leather; the arms a musket and bayonet, the manufacture of Lahore. The cavalry wear helmets or steel caps, round which shawls or scarfs are folded. The *irregulars*, in their dress and appointments, fully justify the appellation which their habits and mode of making war obtained for them. Cotton, silk, or broad cloth tunics of various colours, with the addition of shawls, cloaks, breastplates, or coats of mail, with turban or helmets, *ad libitum*, impart to them a motley but picturesque appearance. They are all badly mounted, and, indeed, little can be said even of the regular cavalry in this respect. The Punjaub breed of horses is far from good, and they do not import stock from other countries to improve their own cattle.

The pay of the *sepoys* of the regular Army of the Punjaub is higher than that of the same class in the Army of the East India Company, each common soldier receiving ten *rupees per mensem*. The troops of the irregulars receive twenty-five *rupees* each, out of which they provide their arms and clothing, and feed their horse, putting the government to no other expense whatever for their services.

Enlistment in the regular Army of the Punjaub is quite voluntary, and the service is so popular that the army could upon an emergency be increased to almost any amount. The soldiery are exceedingly apt in acquiring a knowledge of their military duties; but they are so averse to control that instances of insubordination are common; latterly, indeed, open mutiny has frequently characterised the relations of officer and soldier. Insubordination is punished when punishment is practicable with confinement, loss of pay, or extra duty. But in the present state of military disorganisation no means of chastising rebellion are available.

No pensions were, or are, assigned to the soldiery for long service, nor is there any provision for the widows and families of those who die, or are killed in the service of the state. Promotions, instead of being the right of the good soldier in order of seniority, or the reward of merit in the various grades, is frequently effected by bribery. In the higher ranks, advancement is obtained by the judicious application of *douceurs* to the palm of the favourites at court, or the military chieftains about the person of the sovereign.

In the event of the government of the Punjaub falling into the hands of the British, some time would probably elapse before the dissolute rabble which now composes the army could be brought under a state of as perfect discipline as that which exists in the Anglo-Indian Army; but there is no doubt that ultimately the result of a system, strict and severe from the commencement, when supported by a stern and absolute monarchy, would display itself, and render the Sikh troops as devoted a body as the regular Native Army of Hindostan.

Only twenty-three years, (as at time of publication), have elapsed since the military force in the Punjaub consisted of a large and undisciplined horde. In 1822, the first European officers presented themselves (according to Prinsep) at Runjeet Singh's *durbar*, seeking military service and entertainment. These were Messrs. Allard and Ventura, who had served in the French Army until the annihilation of Napoleon Buonaparte deprived them of employment.

At first, Runjeet Singh, with the suspicion common to a native Indian prince, received them coldly; and his distrust of their purposes was heightened by the Punjaubee chieftains, who were naturally jealous of the introduction of Europeans into the military service; but a submissive and judicious letter from these officers removed the apprehensions of the *maharajah*, and he, with the spirit and originality of a man of genius, admitted them into his service; appointing them instructors of his troops in the European system of drill and warfare. The good conduct and wise management of these gentlemen speedily removed Runjeet Singh's prejudices against Europeans; and the door to employment being thrown open, several military men entered the service of the *maharajah*, and at the close of his reign there were not less than a dozen receiving his pay, and, to use an Indian expression, 'eating his salt.'

The successors of Runjeet Singh, however, did not look with an eye of favour upon men who were not to be bought, and whose sense of personal dignity revolted at the treatment to which the unbridled Sikh chieftains were inclined to subject them. The greater part accordingly resigned their commissions; some of them retiring with ample fortunes, and others seeking honourable employment elsewhere.

The Sikh Army, until lately, was considered by many British officers, who had the opportunity of seeing it, to have been in a fair state of discipline. They form very correct lines, but in manoeuvring their movements are too slow, and they would, in consequence, be in danger, from a body of British cavalry, of being successfully charged during a change of position. They would also run the risk of having their flanks turned by their inability to follow the motion of a European enemy with equal rapidity.

The arms, that is to say, the muskets, are of very inferior stamp, incapable of throwing a ball to any distance, and on quick and repeated discharges liable to burst. Their firing is bad, owing to the very small quantity of practice ammunition allowed by the government; not more than ten balls out of a hundred, at the distance of as many paces, would probably tell upon an enemy's ranks. They still preserve the old system of three ranks, the front one kneeling when firing and then rising to load—a method in action liable to create confusion.

In person, the infantry soldiers are tall and thin, with good features and full beards; their superior height is owing to the extraordinary length of their lower limbs. They are capable of enduring the fatigue of long marches for several days in succession (the author having on one occasion marched with, his regiment a distance of 300 miles within twelve days), and are, generally speaking, so hardy that exposure to oppressive heats or heavy rains has little effect upon them. In a great measure this is the result of custom. Excepting in the vicinity of Lahore and Peshawur, there are few regular quarters or cantonments; the men occupy small tents or *caravanserais*.

The drum and fife and bugle are in general use in the Sikh infantry regiments, and in some of the favourite royal corps of Runjeet Singh an attempt was made to introduce a band of music, but a graft of European melody upon Punjaubee discord did not produce, as may be imagined, a very harmonious result. The cavalry of the Sikh Army is very inferior in every respect to the infantry. While the latter are carefully picked from large bodies of candidates for service, the former are composed of men of all sorts and sizes and ages, who get appointed solely through the interests of the different *sirdars*. They are mean-looking, ill-dressed, and, as already stated, wretchedly mounted. Their horse trappings are of leather of the worst quality, and their saddles are of the same miserable material, and badly constructed. When the horse is in motion, the legs and arms of the rider wave backwards and forwards, right and left, by way, as it were, of keeping time with the pace of the animal bestridden. The horses are small, meagre, and ill-shaped, with the aquiline nose which so peculiarly proclaims inferiority of breed. In the field, the conduct of the Sikh cavalry has generally corresponded with their appearance and efficiency. They are totally deficient of firmness in the hour of struggle, and only charge the foe when a vast superiority of numerical force gives them a sort of warranty of success.

Undeceived touching the supposed weakness of the Sikh Army, Sir Henry Hardinge, in conjunction with his gallant superior in command, Sir Hugh Gough, concentrated his troops, called for reinforcements from the interior, added largely to his commissariat—and what in Eastern warfare is altogether indispensable, largely increased his beasts of burden and means of transport. Then taking a central position, he waited calmly and prudently until the Sikh designs should be more clearly developed.

November came; the storm had been gathering; remonstrances from the governor-general had failed; and on the 4th, the Sikh *vakeel* was formally dismissed. Still immediate hostilities were not anticipated, when suddenly news arrived on the 13th, that the enemy had crossed the Sutlej, and Ferozepore was invested. The British commander hurried by forced marches to its relief, and on the 18th, after a seven leagues' march, at noon the Anglo-Indian Army reached the village of Moodkee. A movement of twenty miles under an eastern sun is most distressing, and the wearied troops having bivouacked, ignorant of the proximity of an enemy, cut wood, lighted fires, and commenced cooking. Strange as it may appear, although in the immediate presence of the Sikh Army, no vidette had seen it, and the booming of the enemy's guns first gave note of preparation.

The army was in a state of great exhaustion, principally from the want of water, which was not procurable on the road, when about 3 p.m., information was received that the Sikh Army was advancing; and the troops had scarcely time to get under arms and move to their positions, when that fact was ascertained.

Lord Gough says:—

I immediately pushed forward the horse artillery and cavalry, directing the infantry, accompanied by the field batteries, to move forward in support. We had not proceeded beyond two miles, when we found the enemy in position. They were said to consist of from 15,000 to 20,000 infantry, about the same force of cavalry, and forty guns. They evidently had either just taken up this position, or were advancing in order of battle against us. To resist their attack and to cover the formation of the infantry, I advanced the cavalry under Brigadiers White, Gough, and Mactier, rapidly to the front, in columns of squadrons, and occupied the plain. They were speedily followed by the five troops of horse artillery, under Brigadier Brooke, who took up a forward position, having the cavalry then on his flanks.

The country is a dead flat, covered at short intervals with a low, but in some places, thick *jhow* jungle and dotted with sandy hillocks. The enemy screened their infantry and artillery behind this jungle, and such undulations as the ground afforded; and, whilst our twelve battalions formed from echelon of brigade into line, opened a very serious cannonade upon our advancing troops, which was vigorously replied to by the battery of horse artillery under Brigadier Brooke, which was soon joined by the two light field batteries.

The rapid and well-directed fire of our artillery appeared soon to paralyse that of the enemy, and, as it was necessary to complete our infantry dispositions without advancing the artillery too near to the jungle, I directed the cavalry under Brigadiers White and Gough to make a flank movement on the enemy's left, with a view of threatening and turning that flank, if possible. With praiseworthy gallantry, the 3rd Light Dragoons, with the 2nd brigade of cavalry, consisting of the bodyguard and fifth Light Cavalry, with a portion of the 4th Lancers, turned the left of the Sikh Army, and, sweeping along the whole rear of its infantry and guns, silenced for a time the latter, and put their numerous cavalry to flight.

Whilst this movement was taking place on the enemy's left, I directed the remainder of the 4th Lancers, the 9th Irregular Cavalry, under Brigadier Mactier, with, a light field battery, to threaten their right. This manoeuvre was also successful. Had not the infantry and guns of the enemy been screened by the jungle, these brilliant charges of the cavalry would have been productive of greater effect.

When the infantry advanced to the attack, Brigadier Brooke rapidly pushed on his horse artillery close to the jungle, and the cannonade was resumed on both sides. The infantry, under Major-Generals Sir Harry Smith, Gilbert, and Sir John Mc-Caskill, attacked in echelon of lines the enemy's infantry, almost invisible amongst the wood and the approaching darkness of night. The opposition of the enemy was such as might have been expected from troops who had everything at stake, and who had long vaunted of being irresistible. Their ample and extended line, from their great superiority of numbers, far outflanked ours; but this was counteracted by the flank movement of our cavalry.

The attack of the infantry now commenced; and the roll of fire from this powerful arm soon convinced the Sikh Army that they had met with a foe they little expected; and their whole force was driven from position after position, with great slaughter, and the loss of seventeen pieces of artillery, some of them of heavy calibre; our infantry using that never-failing weapon, the bayonet, whenever the enemy stood. Night only saved them from worse disaster, for this stout conflict was maintained during an hour and a half of the dim starlight, amidst a cloud of dust from the sandy plain, which yet more obscured every object.

I regret to say this gallant and successful attack was attended with considerable loss; the force bivouacked upon the field for some hours, and only returned to its encampment after ascertaining that it had no enemy before it, and night prevented the possibility of a regular advance in pursuit.

In this brilliant and sanguinary battle, the British loss was necessarily heavy. Sir Robert Sale, and Sir John McCaskill were killed, and Brigadiers Bolton. and Mactier, with Colonels Byrne and Bunbury wounded. The total casualties amounted to 872 of all arms.

Nothing could have been more fortunate than the prestige which Moodkee gave to the campaign. One damning fault of the Spanish generals on the Peninsula was that they literally over-marched their troops until they came to a dead standstill—and this the British commanders most judiciously avoided.

There was great suffering everywhere for want of water. Hunger men may endure for days together; but a burning thirst in a tropical climate is terrible; and when the fever in the blood becomes aggravated by such exertions as the British Army had that day made, the whole world seems valueless in comparison with a cup of cold water. None came, however, for several hours; yet the gallant fellows bore the privation without a murmur; and when the following day brought them a reinforcement of two European regiments of infantry, with a small battery of heavy guns, they felt that they were irresistible. Nevertheless, the general, with great good sense, gave them two entire days to refresh; he had nothing to gain by precipitating matters.

Ferozepore had been saved by the battle of the 18th, and his communications with the place being in some sort restored, he had time to warn Sir John Littler of his purposes, and to prepare him for co-operating in their accomplishment. These were the chief advantages of delay; besides that, others probably occurred to him, namely, the opportunity which was afforded for the coming up of the corps which had been directed to march from Delhi, Meerut, and other stations. And on the part of the Sikhs, it was doubtless considered that their very numbers would render a long halt on one spot impossible for them; for no country, however fertile, can sustain the pressure of sixty thousand men many days.

A little delay in active operations was, under circumstances, particularly politic, for while the Sikhs were shaken in confidence and marvelling at their discomfiture, the British lion was gathering strength to make another and a deadlier spring.

CHAPTER 7

The Battle of Ferozepore: 1845

On the morning of the 21st, the Anglo-Indian Army again took the offensive, and marched against the entrenched position of the enemy, and the details of the succeeding events of that bloody and glorious day are thus lucidly and modestly given still by Lord Gough.

Instead of advancing to the direct attack of their formidable works, our force manoeuvred to their right; the second and fourth divisions of infantry, in front, supported by the first division and cavalry in second line, continued to defile for some time out of cannon-shot between the Sikhs and Ferozepore. The desired effect was not long delayed, a cloud of dust was seen on our left, and according to the instructions sent him on the preceding evening, Major-General Sir John Littler, with his division, availing himself of the offered opportunity, was discovered in full march to unite his force with mine. The junction was soon effected, and thus was accomplished one of the great objects of all our harassing marches and privations, in the relief of this division of our army from the blockade of the numerous forces by which it was surrounded.

Dispositions were now made for a united attack on the enemy's entrenched camp. We found it to be a parallelogram of about a mile in length and half a mile in breadth, including within its area the strong village of Ferozeshah; the shorter sides looking towards the Sutlej and Moodkee, and the longer towards Ferozepore and the open country. We moved against the last named face, the ground in front of which was, like the Sikh position in Moodkee, covered with low jungle.

The divisions of Major-General Sir John Littler, Brigadier Wallace (who had succeeded Major-General Sir John McCaskill), and Major-General Gilbert, deployed into line, having in the centre our whole force of artillery, with the exception of three troops of horse artillery, one on either flank, and one in support, to be moved as occasion required. Major-General Sir Harry Smith's division, and our small cavalry force, moved in second line, having a brigade in reserve to cover each wing.

I should here observe that I committed the charge and direction of the left wing to Lieutenant-General Sir Henry Hardinge, while I personally conducted the right.

A very heavy cannonade was opened by the enemy, who had dispersed over their position upwards of 100 guns, more than 40 of which were of battering calibre; these kept up a heavy and well-directed fire, which the practice of our far less numerous artillery, of much lighter metal, checked in some degree, but could not silence; finally, in the face of a storm of shot and shell, our infantry advanced and carried these formidable entrenchments; they threw themselves upon the guns, and with matchless gallantry wrested them from the enemy; but, when the batteries were partially within our grasp, our soldiery had to face such a fire of musketry from the Sikh infantry, arrayed behind their guns, that, in spite of the most heroic efforts, a portion only of the entrenchment could be carried. Night fell while the conflict was everywhere raging.

Although I now brought up Major-General Sir Harry Smith's division, and he captured and long retained another point of the position, and Her Majesty's 3rd Light Dragoons charged and took some of the most formidable batteries, yet the enemy remained in possession of a considerable portion of the great quadrangle, whilst our troops, intermingled with theirs, kept possession of the remainder, and finally bivouacked upon it, exhausted by their gallant efforts, greatly reduced in numbers, and suffering extremely from thirst, yet animated by an indomitable spirit. In this state of things, the long night wore away.

Near the middle of it one of their heavy guns was advanced, and played with deadly effect upon our troops. Lieutenant-General Sir Henry Hardinge immediately formed Her Majesty's 80th Foot and the 1st European Light Infantry. They were led to the attack by their commanding officers, and animated in their exertions by Lieutenant-Colonel Wood (*aide-de-camp* to the

BATTLE OF FEROZESHAH

lieutenant-general), who was wounded in the onset. The 80th captured the gun, and the enemy, dismayed by this counter-check, did not venture to press on further. During the whole night, however, they continued to harass our troops by fire of artillery, wherever moonlight discovered our position.

But with daylight of the 22nd came retribution. Our infantry formed line, supported on both flanks by horse artillery, whilst a fire was opened from our centre by such of our heavy guns as remained effective, aided by a flight of rockets. A masked battery player! with great effect upon this point, dismounting our pieces, and blowing up our tumbrils. At this moment, Lieutenant-General Sir Henry Hardinge placed himself at the head of the left, whilst I rode at the head of the right wing.

Our line advanced, and, unchecked by the enemy's fire, drove them rapidly out of the village of Ferozeshah and their encampment; then, changing front to its left, on its centre, our force continued to sweep the camp, bearing down all opposition, and dislodged the enemy from their whole position. The line then halted, as if on a day of manoeuvre, receiving its two leaders as they rode along its front with a gratifying cheer, and displaying the captured standards of the Khalsa Army. We had taken upwards of seventy-three pieces of cannon, and were masters of the whole field.

The force assumed a position on the ground which it had won, but even here its labours were not to cease. In the course of two hours, Sirdar Tej Singh, who had commanded in the last great battle, brought up from the vicinity of Ferozepore fresh battalions and a large field of artillery, supported by 30,000 Ghorepurras, hitherto encamped near the river.

He drove in our cavalry parties, and made strenuous efforts to regain the position of Ferozeshah; this attempt was defeated, but its failure had scarcely become manifest when the *sirdar* renewed the contest with more troops and a large artillery. He commenced by a combination against our left flank; and when this was frustrated, made such a demonstration against the captured villages as compelled us to change our whole front to the right. His guns during this manoeuvre maintained an incessant fire, whilst our artillery ammunition being completely expended in these protracted combats, we were unable to answer him with a single shot.

I now directed our almost exhausted cavalry to threaten both flanks at once, preparing the infantry to advance in support, which apparently caused him suddenly to cease his fire and abandon the field.

For twenty-four hours, not a Sikh has appeared in our front. The remains of the Khalsa Army are said to be in full retreat across the Sutlej, at Nuggurputhur and Tella, or marching up its left bank towards Hurreekeeputhur, in the greatest confusion and dismay. Of their chiefs, Bahadur Singh is killed, Lai Singh said to be wounded, Mehtab Singh, Adjoodhia Pershad, and Tej Singh, the late governor of Peshawur, have fled with precipitation. Their camp is the scene of the most awful carnage, and they have abandoned large stores of grain, camp equipage, and ammunition.

Thus, has apparently terminated this unprovoked and criminal invasion of the peaceful provinces under British protection.

On the conclusion of such a narrative as I have given, it is surely superfluous in me to say that I am, and shall be to the last moment of my existence, proud of the army which I had to command on the 21st and 22nd instant. To their gallant exertions I owe the satisfaction of seeing such a victory achieved, and the glory of having my own name associated with it.

The loss of this army has been heavy; how could a hope be formed that it should be otherwise?

★★★★★★★★★★

Killed.—European officers, 37; native officers, 17; non-commissioned, drummers, rank and file. 630; *syces*, drivers, &c., 10. Total, 694.

Wounded.—European officers, 78; native officers, 18; non-commissioned, drummers, rank and file, 1,610; *syces*, drivers, &c., 12: warrant officers, 3. Total, 1,721,

Grand total of all ranks killed and wounded, 2,415.

★★★★★★★★★★

Within thirty hours this force stormed an entrenched camp, fought a general action, and sustained two considerable combats with the enemy. Within four days it has dislodged from their positions, on the left bank of the Sutlej, 60,000 Sikh soldiers, supported by upwards of 150 pieces of cannon, 108 of which the enemy acknowledge to have lost, and 91 of which are in our possession.

In addition to our losses in the battle, the captured camp was found to be everywhere protected by charged mines, by the successive springing of which many brave officers and men have been destroyed.

These glorious battles were within a month followed up by that of Aliwal—as sanguinary an affair as either of its predecessors, and, in a military point of view, decidedly more scientific in arrangement and execution. In one operation, it seemed a pendant to the beautiful movement on the retreat from Burgos, when Wellington carried his army bodily round Souham's and placed the French general in the afternoon in the same unfavourable position in which he (Wellington) had found himself that morning. The action had not been expected, for the service required had been effected without resistance.

CHAPTER 8

The Battles of Aliwal and Sobraon: 1846

Though the treaty which held the British and Sikh Governments
in amity provided that the Sikhs should send no troops across the
Sutlej, they were permitted to retain certain *jaghires*, or feudal possessions, on the left bank, one of which comprised the town and fort of
Dheerrumcote. Here the enemy had established a magazine of grain;
and a small garrison, consisting of mercenaries, chiefly Rohillas and
Afghans, were thrown into the place for its protection. But besides
that, the grain was needed in the British lines, the presence of a hostile
garrison on his own side of the stream was an eyesore and an annoy-
ance, to the British general; and Major-General Sir Harry Smith was
directed with a brigade of infantry and a few guns, to reduce it.

He accomplished the service on the 18th of January without loss,
or, indeed, sustaining a serious resistance; and was on his way back to
camp, when tidings reached the commander-in-chief of a nature not
to be dealt lightly with, far less neglected.

It was ascertained that the enemy had detached 20,000 men from
their camp at Sobraon against Loodiana. Their objects were repre-
sented to be, not only the seizure of that place, but the interruption of
the British communications with the rear, and, perhaps, the capture of
the battering-train, which was advancing by Busseean; and Sir Harry
Smith, being reinforced to the amount of 8,000 men, received instructions to counterwork the project. His business was to form a junction
with Colonel Godby, who, with one regiment of cavalry, and four of
infantry, occupied Loodiana; and then, and not till then, to push the
Sikhs, and drive them, if possible, back upon their own country.

Here again, the school in which he had been taught his trade was
evidence in the conduct of the commander, who proved in his hour
of trial that Peninsular instruction had not been thrown away. The
Sikhs had already shut the garrison of Loodiana in; burned a new bar-

71

rack, and ravaged the surrounding country. A creeping commander now would have been found wanting; but Smith was a man of different mettle, and, pushing rapidly on, a clean march brought him within twenty-five miles of Loodiana, and with the *réveil*, he resumed his movement next morning.

At Buddewal the enemy showed himself, occupying a connected line of villages in front, and covered by a powerful artillery. To gain his object and reach Loodiana, it was necessary for Sir Harry Smith to change his order of march, and while the Sikhs, who had already outflanked him, opened a fire of forty guns on the advancing columns, Smith massed his weak artillery, and under its concentrated and well-directed cannonade, broke into echelons, and threatened the Sikh front, the while making a flank movement by his right, protected *en échelon* by the cavalry. Nothing could be more beautifully and successfully executed than this delicate manoeuvre. Sir Harry carried his guns and baggage round the enemy—a small portion only of the latter passing into the temporary possession of the Sikhs.

Colonel Godby, who commanded the invested garrison, having seen the cloud of dust, moved from Loodiana; and marching parallel to the direction which it seemed to take, found himself in due time connected by his patrols with Smith's advanced guard. Both corps upon this placed themselves with Loodiana in their rear, and the enemy before them; the latter being so circumstanced that the British Army lay, as it were, upon one of its flanks. But Smith, though he had thus relieved the town, was unwilling to strike a blow till he could make it decisive. He, therefore, encamped in an attitude of watchfulness, waiting till another brigade should arrive, which, under the command of Colonel Wheeler, was marching from headquarters to reinforce him.

Colonel Wheeler's march, seems to have been conducted with equal diligence and care. He heard of the encounter of the 21st, and of its results; whereupon he abandoned the direct road to Loodiana, and following a circuitous route, went round the enemy's position, without once coming under fire. He reached Sir Harry Smith's camp in safety; and, on the 26th, Smith made his preparations to fight a great battle. But it was found, ere the columns were put in motion, that the enemy had abandoned their position at Buddewal, and were withdrawn to an entrenched camp nearer to the river, of which the village of Aliwal was the key, covering the ford by which they had crossed, and on which they depended, in the event of a reverse, as a line of

BATTLE OF SOBRAON

retreat. Operations were accordingly suspended, and such further arrangements set going as the altered state of affairs seemed to require.

On the 27th, Runjoor Singh having been reinforced by Avitabile's brigade, 4,000 Sikh regulars, some cavalry, and twelve guns, found himself, as he had reason to believe, in a condition to deliver battle; and to intercept the Anglo-Indian communications, he advanced towards Ingraon, where, early on the 28th, Sir Harry Smith found himself in position. His right rested on a height, his left on a field entrenchment, while his centre held ground in the immediate front of the: village of Aliwal (or Ulleéwal). The Anglo-Indian Army amounted to some 12,000 men of all arms; the Sikhs doubled them in numerical strength, and that too was composed of the flower of their army.

The subsequent details of this glorious action may be rapidly described. Smith boldly advanced against the Sikh position, under a heavy cannonade, while the right brigades were getting into line. The advance was splendid—the British cavalry driving the Sikh horsemen on their infantry, forced the left back, capturing several guns, while on the left of the British line the Ayeen brigade (Avitabile's) were deforced, and the village of Bhoondi, where the right of the Sikhs endeavoured to make a stand, was carried with the bayonet. A general rout ensued, the enemy pressing in confused masses towards the ford, while every attempt they made to rally was anticipated by a charge, and the destruction of the flower of the Sikh Army was completed.

The firing began about ten in the morning; by one o'clock in the day the Sikh Army was broken and routed, the ground covered with its wreck, and the Sutlej choked with the dead and the dying. The whole of the artillery, fifty-seven guns, fell into the hands of the victors, and the booty was immense; but the victors had neither time nor inclination to dwell upon their triumphs. There was no further danger to be apprehended here. Of the 24,000 men who, in the morning, threatened Loodiana, scarcely as many hundreds held together; and these, after a brief show of rally on the opposite bank, melted away and disappeared entirely.

Having bivouacked that night, therefore, on the field which he had won, and sent in the wounded, with the captured guns, under sufficient escort, to Loodiana, Sir Harry Smith, with the bulk of his division, took the road to headquarters; and, in the afternoon of the 8th of February, came into position on the right of the main army, which was his established post.

In this most glorious battle, the Anglo-Indian Army had 151 men

Battle of Aliwal

killed, 413 wounded, and 25 missing a loss comparatively small.

The immediate consequences of the victory of Aliwal, was the evacuation of the left bank of the Sutlej by the enemy. The Sikhs had sustained three terrible defeats; they had lost an enormous quantity of military *matériel*, 150 guns, and none could presume to estimate the number of their best and bravest troops who had been placed *hors de combat*. In hundreds the slaughtered and drowned victims at Aliwal floated to Sobraon with the stream; but still with a *tête de pont* to secure their bridge communications with the right bank and the reserve there, formidable entrenchments, armed with seventy heavy guns, and 30,000 of their best troops (the Khalsa), they determined to defend them, boldly held their ground, and dared another battle.

On being rejoined by Sir Harry Smith's division, and having receive his siege-train and a supply of ammunition from Delhi, the commander-in-chief and the governor-general determined to force the Sikh position. Unopposed they gained possession of Little Sobraon and Kodeewalla, and both, the field batteries and heavy guns were planted to throw a concentrated fire upon the entrenchments occupied by the enemy. Close to the river bank, Dick's division was stationed to assault the Sikh right, while another brigade was held in reserve behind the village of Kodeewalla.

In the centre, Gilbert's division was formed, either for attack or support, its right flank applied on the village of Little Sobraon. Smith's division took ground near the village of Guttah, with its right inclining towards the Sutlej; Cureton's brigade observed the ford at Hurree, and held Lal Singh's horsemen in check; the remainder of the cavalry, under Major-General Thackwell, acting in reserve.

The British batteries opened a lively cannonade soon after sunrise, but guns in field position have little chance of silencing artillery covered by strong redoubts. At nine, the attack commenced by Stacy's brigade of Dick's division, advancing against the enemy's entrenchments. The crushing fire of the Sikh guns would have arrested the advance of any but most daring regiments, but the brigadier pressed gallantly on, and while the British bayonet met the Mussulman sabre the camp was carried. The sappers broke openings in the entrenching mounds, through which, although in single files, the cavalry pushed, reformed, and charged. The Sikh gunners were sabred in their batteries, while the entire of the infantry and every disposable gun were promptly brought into action by Sir Hugh Gough.

The Sikh fire became more feeble, their best battalions unsteady, and the British pressed boldly on. Wavering troops rarely withstand a struggle when the bayonet comes into play, and the Khalsas broke entirely, and hurried from the field to the river and bridge. But the hour of retributive vengeance had arrived, and the waters of the Sutlej offered small protection to the fugitives. The stream had risen, the fords were unsafe, and flying from the fire of the horse-artillery, which had opened on the mobbed fugitives with grape shot, hundreds fell under this murderous cannonade, while thousands found a grave in the no longer friendly waters of their native rivers, until it almost excited the compassion, of an irritated enemy.

At every point the entrenchments were carried. The horse artillery galloped through, and both they and the batteries opened such a fire upon the broken enemy as swept them away by ranks. "The fire of the Sikhs," says the commander-in-chief, "first slackened, and then nearly ceased; and the victors then pressing them on every side, precipitated them over the bridge into the Sutlej, which a sudden rise of seven inches had rendered hardly fordable." The awful slaughter, confusion, and dismay were such as would have excited compassion in the hearts of their conquerors, if the Khalsa troops had not, in the early part of the action, sullied their gallantry by slaughtering and barbarously mangling every wounded soldier whom, in the vicissitudes of attack, the fortune of war left at their mercy.

At Sobraon, the final blow which extinguished the military power of the Sikhs, was delivered. Sixty-seven pieces of artillery, two hundred camel-guns, standards, tumbrils, ammunition, camp equipage—in a word, all that forms the *matériel* of an army in the field, fell into the hands of the victors. In native armies, no regular returns of the killed and wounded are made out, but the Sikh losses were computed at 8,000 men, and the amount was not exaggerated.

On the bloody height of Sobraon the Sikh War virtually terminated, for, on that evening, the Anglo-Indian Army commenced their march upon Lahore. Frightfully defeated, and humbled to the dust, the once haughty chiefs sent *vakeels* to implore mercy from the conqueror. The ambassadors, however, were refused an audience, and it was intimated that the British generals would condescend to treat with none except the *maharajah* in person.

Trembling for his capital, which nothing but abject submission now could save, the youthful monarch, attended by Rajah Goolab Singh, repaired to the British camp. Stringent terms were most justly exacted, and while the rich district between the Sutlej and the Beeas, and what were termed "the Protected States," were ceded for ever to Britain, a million and a half sterling was agreed to by the Sikh *durbar*, as compensation for the expenditure of the war, while the Punjaub should remain in military occupation until the full amount should be discharged.

CHAPTER 9

The Battle of Martaban: 1852

The treaty of Yundaboo concluded the Burmese War of 1824. By its terms, the safety of British commerce and British merchants in Burmah was assured, and for a long period following the termination of the war the terms of the treaty were rigidly adhered to. By degrees, however, a spirit of resentment against the British began to spring up in the only half-civilised country, and in 1851 such resentment found open expression.

In the course of that year, a Mr. Sheppard, the master and owner of a trading vessel of Madras, complained to the Indian Government that he had been seized, ill-treated, and imprisoned by the Governor of Rangoon, upon a false charge of throwing a man overboard, that his vessel had been detained, and over a thousand *rupees* extorted from him; adding that this was one of many acts of injustice, oppression, and tyranny suffered by British subjects in that port. Shortly after, another master of a British ship made a similar complaint, alleging that he had been subjected to extortions, as well as insult and indignity, by the governor, on an equally false charge of murdering one of his crew.

At the same time a memorial was sent from the merchants of Rangoon to the Governor-General of India, in which they alleged that they had, for a long time, suffered from the tyranny of the Burmese authorities, that trade was seriously obstructed, and that neither life nor property was safe, as the governor had publicly stated to his dependants that he had no more money to give them, and had granted them his permission to get money as they could; that he had frequently demanded money without any pretext, and tortured the parties asked until his demands were complied with, and that, in short, affairs had arrived at such a crisis that, unless protected, the British merchants in Rangoon would be obliged to leave the country.

After careful consideration, the governor-general came to the conclusion that the treaty of Yundaboo had been unquestionably set at nought, that gross injustice and oppression had been perpetrated, and that the court of Ava should make due reparation. Accordingly, Commodore Lambert, with H.M.S. *Fox* and two other steamers, was at once despatched to Rangoon to enforce this demand of the Indian Government, and to present a letter to the King of Ava setting forth the government's grounds for the taking of such a step.

Arrived at Rangoon, Captain Tarleton, with other officers, landed to present this letter for the king to the governor of the port. His reception was insulting in the extreme, and an account of the proceedings having been forwarded to the Indian Government, a further and more emphatic "note" was sent. On receipt of this second letter, amendment was promised to the Indian authorities. "The Great English War-Chiefs" were informed that strict inquiry would be made into affairs, just treatment should be accorded the merchants, and that a fresh governor would be appointed.

This step was taken, but the incoming governor "chastised with scorpions," instead of with the "whips" of his predecessor, and things rapidly went from bad to worse. A climax was reached when Commodore Lambert sent Captain Fishbourne of H.M.S. *Hermes* with a letter stating the precise claims of the Indian Government. Captain Fishbourne was informed that the governor was asleep, which was not true, and that they must wait in an open shed until he awoke and could receive them. After remaining for some little time, they returned to the ship without having been admitted to the governor's presence.

Commodore Lambert's reply to this latest insult was short and sharp. He seized a vessel belonging to the King of Ava, declared the river mouth to be in a state of blockade, and invited all persons in Rangoon who claimed British protection to come aboard his ship. Four days later, on the 10th January, 1852, a brisk cannonade was opened on the *Fox* from a stockade on the adjacent river bank. A few rounds from the British vessel sufficed to silence the battery, and immediately afterwards the *Fox* returned to Calcutta to report the state of affairs.

The next move in the Burmese situation took the form of a lengthy and formal remonstrance to the King of Ava, once more demanding reparation. Regret was to be expressed for former discourtesies; ten *lacs* of *rupees* were demanded in compensation; a respectful reception was solicited for the incoming representative of the British Government; and finally, the removal the obnoxious were demanded as terms

BATTLE OF MARTABAN

by which alone peace could be maintained.

If without further delay, negotiation, or correspondence, these conditions shall be consented to, and shall be fulfilled by the 1st April next, hostile operations shall be stayed

Failing this, war would be declared.

The guilt and consequences of such war will rest upon the head of the ruler of Ava.

In answer to this ultimatum, no concession was made by the Burmese, and a hostile expedition was at once prepared.

The armament was to consist of troops from the Presidencies of Bengal and Madras, with the 18th Royal Irish, 35th Royal Sussex, the 51st Light Infantry, and the Staffordshire regiment. The whole force, some 4400 of all ranks, was placed under the command of Major-General Godwin, a veteran officer who was engaged in the first Burmese war. The conditions of peace were specified at the outset. Fifteen *lacs* of *rupees* were demanded for expenses, with an additional three *lacs* for every month after the 1st May. Until these payments were made, the British troops were to remain in possession of such places as they might capture.

General Godwin set sail with his forces on the 28th March, and reached Rangoon on the 2nd April, where he found Rear-Admiral Austin, C.B., the naval commander-in-chief, who had come from Penang in H.M.S. *Rattler*. Martaban, which had a river line of defences about 800 yards in length, was at once selected as the first objective of attack.

Arrangements were made for the attack on daybreak of the 5th April. The admiral made every disposition possible, "in waters full of shoals and violent currents," for bombarding the position with his five steamers, and to cover the landing of the troops. General Godwin's official narrative runs:—

It was the admiration of everyone, to witness the noble manner in which the *Rattler* worked her way within 200 yards of the wall and close to the *pagoda*, doing tremendous execution, I changed from the *Rattler* at six o'clock, to superintend the landing of the troops, and went on board a smaller vessel, the *Proserpine*, with my staff. At half-past six the steamer opened fire, and at seven the troops were in the boats, and landed, by the indefatigable exertions of Commander Brooking, under a smart fire of musketry and guns. Soon was the storming party under the walls and over them, with less loss than I thought possible. Lieutenant-Colonel Reignolds immediately ascended to the *pagodas* on the height, and took possession of them after some skirmishing with the enemy. At eight a.m. Martaban was won, and, considering the enemy's position and numbers, which report gives at 5,000 men, we have got it very cheaply.

Thus, tersely is the account of the first engagement of the war rendered. By the 9th, the expedition lay off Rangoon, the principal port on the eastern branch of the Irrawaddy. Occasional patches of forest and rice flats surround the Burmese capital from the midst of whose wooden houses rose, in those days, the Great Pagoda, a religious edifice of both literal and figurative high-standing. Three hundred and fifty feet has been given as the height of this edifice, and not only was it surrounded by stockades and cannon, but, if reports were true, its interior was loaded with vast treasure, which would make its capture a profitable as well as honourable enterprise.

Not until Wednesday, the 14th April, were preparations fully completed for the assault on the Great Pagoda, but the two preceding days were spent in several severe skirmishes with the enemy. On the 12th, a party landed from the 51st Light Infantry, Royal Irish, and Bengal Infantry met with stout opposition from the Burmese, who had entrenched themselves behind a stockade. After a heavy artillery fire, the place was carried by assault, but with heavy loss to our forces. The heat was terrific. By 11 a.m. the sun assumed such power that Major Oakes was killed by sunstroke while working his battery, Major Griffith died from the same cause in the act of carrying an order, and Colonel Foord was compelled to leave the field of action.

The next day was spent in further landing operations, and on the morning of the 14th the troops moved forward to the grand assault.

About three-quarters of a mile separated the Great Pagoda from the south entrance of Rangoon, whence our troops were advancing. The old road from the river to the *pagoda* came up from the south gate, and it was apparently by this; road the Burmese decided that the British assault would come. Here they had placed the enormous number of 100 pieces of cannon and a garrison of at least 10,000 men; but, perceiving their extensive dispositions, the British commander decided on another plan of attack.

The troops were under arms at 5 a.m., "all in as fine a temper as ever men were." The route lay to the north-west through thick jungle. Four light guns, 9-pounders, their flanks protected by two companies of the 80th regiment, the rest of the wing of that corps following with two more guns; the 18th Royal Irish, and the 40th Bengal Native Infantry formed the advance. The 51st Light Infantry and the Madras troops formed the reserve.

After a mile's march, the troops came in full view of the *pagoda*, which immediately opened fire. Very soon, however, under a galling fire from two guns served by Major Montgomery of the Madras Artillery, the enemy's flank was turned, and a strong position taken up by our artillery on the east side of the *pagoda*. Some time was however spent in bringing up the guns, an operation in which the naval brigade from the *Fox* rendered invaluable assistance, and meantime the enemy's fire wrought terrible havoc in our ranks. Sunstroke, as formerly, was also severely depleting the British forces.

So hot, indeed, became the Burmese fire, that the general now determined on an immediate assault. Captain Laller, the interpreter, assured the British commander that he could effectively lead a storming party through the eastern gate, and this bold and enterprising plan was at once adopted.

The storming party was formed of the wing of the 80th regiment, under Major Lockhart; two companies of the Royal Irish, under Lieutenant Hewitt; and two companies of the 40th Bengal Native Infantry, under Lieutenant White Lieutenant-Colonel Coote being in charge of the entire party.

Under a heavy fire from cannon and musket, and led forward by Captain Laller, sword in hand, the storming party swept forward. The eight hundred yards which separated our position from the walls of the *pagoda* was crossed in a twinkling, and, with a loud cheer, the eastern gate of the temple was burst in, and, with ball and bayonet, the Burmese were driven from their entrenched position.

The British loss was heavy. Lieutenant Doran, of the Royal Irish, fell mortally wounded, four bullets being found in his body; Colonel Coote himself was struck, and many were the dead and dying who strewed the steep steps of the *pagoda*,

General Godwin says:—

When the storming party reached the steps, a tremendous rush was made to the upper terrace, and deafening cheers told that the *pagoda* no longer belonged to the Burmese.

The enemy ran in confusion from the southern and western gates, where they were met by the fire from the steamers. Among the first to flee was the governor, who, with his bodyguard in tall gilt hats, beat a hasty and ignominious retreat.

Of seventeen killed on the British side, three were officers, two others dying of sunstroke. The wounded numbered 132. Casualties in the fleet were 17 in all. The number of Burmese dead was never accurately ascertained, but it was considerable. Ninety cannon and nearly as many wall pieces were captured.

The general's report ran:

All the country round has fallen with the *pagoda*.

On the 19th May the town of Bassan, on the river of that name, was captured by the British troops after a sharp struggle. After leaving a small garrison in the place, General Godwin returned to Rangoon there to organise arrangements for his main advance.

CHAPTER 10

The Battle of Pegu: 1852

The next event of importance in this campaign was the desperate attack made by the Burmese on Martaban, to recover the town which they had lost. On the 26th May, upwards of a thousand Burmese made a violent onslaught upon the British troops in occupation. Major Hall of the 49th Madras Light Infantry was in command, and, after some pretty severe fighting, during which three men of a reconnoitring party were killed, the artillery were brought into action with deadly effect, and the foe driven back.

Says one account:—

The British cannon-balls made literal lanes in the seething masses of Burmese, crushing many to atoms, and dismembering others who were unlucky enough to be in their track.

The discomfiture of the enemy was subsequently largely augmented by shot and shell from the British war vessels, and a total rout of the attacking party was the result. Martaban was thus securely retained in British hands; but the war was far from being over.

Early in July, Captain Tarleton, R.N., was ordered to ascend the Irrawaddy with five steamers and reconnoitre the position and defences of the Burmese in the vicinity of Prome. This town of wooden houses is about a mile and a half in circumference, and lies on the left bank of the river. It is surrounded by low-lying swamps which at times are inundated by the overflow of the Irrawaddy. At a short distance from the city the river divides itself into two streams—the left, or western, being the deeper, and the only one navigable, except in the heart of the rainy season.

On the left bank of the navigable branch of the stream Captain Tarleton soon decried a force of nearly 10,000 Burmese, who from a strongly-fortified bastion were preparing to oppose his advance up the left branch of the river. Eagerly the Burmese watched the approach of the British gunboat, which they believed would shortly be at their mercy, as it steamed steadily forward towards the left branch of the river, where their cannon and musketry were already trained to receive it. Captain Tarleton, however, had no intention of being caught in the trap. Realising the enemy's strength, he resolved to risk his vessel, which was of light draught, in the waters of the eastern branch of the stream, aware that at the rainy season it would be navigable for at least some distance.

Such, indeed, proved to be the case, and, to the astonishment of the crowds of baffled Burmese onlookers, the little craft plunged boldly up the eastern water, and was very soon out of range of their cannon. A few shot indeed reached the British vessel, but no damage was done, and Prome was reached on the 9th without further opposition. Here it was found that no garrison had been left in charge, and after carrying off some guns, and spiking others, and destroying all the enemy's stores they could lay hands on, the expedition returned to Rangoon.

On the return journey the main Burmese Army was encountered crossing the parent stream of the Irrawaddy, and a heavy cannonade was opened by the British on the confused mass as it performed its clumsy evolutions. Not only the state barge of the Burmese general fell into our hands, but between 40 and 50 boats containing stores and munitions of war, which were destroyed. After nine days' absence, Captain Tarleton returned to Rangoon in triumph, well satisfied with the result of his reconnoitring operations.

On the 27th July, Lord Dalhousie, the Governor-General of India, arrived at Rangoon on a brief visit, and expressed his great satisfaction with the work of the troops.

Not until the 16th September were any more extensive operations conducted by General Godwin, the interval being spent in collecting munitions of war and transport material, and, by the gunboats, in patrolling the river between Rangoon and Prome. On the date mentioned, however, the embarkation began, with Prome as the objective. On the morning of the 9th October the expedition came in sight of Prome, and the war vessels anchored in the small bay which lies opposite the town. Towards evening the troops were landed. A suburb to the north of Prome, and outside the town, was chosen as the point of debarkation, as it was known that the enemy were in force further to the south.

The landing was opposed by the Burmese with musket and *gingal*.

From some of the wooden houses of the suburb, from the adjacent jungle, and from a small *pagoda* which faced the immediate path of the troops, a fierce musket fire was poured upon the attacking force, and so hot did this become that it became necessary to dislodge the unseen assailants. Brigadier Reignolds, with Captains Christie and Welsh, with several companies of the 80th regiment, were quickly sent forward to rush the foe from their position—an operation which they performed with great gallantry and with every success, one man only being killed in the attack.

The captured *pagoda* was retained by our men for the night, the enemy not returning to the attack. In the morning the landing was completed, and, on a general advance being made, it was found that the enemy had been so severely handled in the engagement of the previous evening that they had evacuated the place, "leaving in our possession a town overrun with thick and rank vegetation and abounding in swamps."

Says General Godwin of the position of our troops at this stage of the war:—

I have been for a long time aware of the assemblage of a large force of troops about ten miles east of Prome nearly 18,000 men, well posted in two or more stockades. It is not my intention to disturb them in any way at present, as, by their concentration at that point, the fine force now assembling here will have an opportunity of striking a blow which may put an end to much future opposition.

Accordingly, a different scene of operations was next chosen. The Burmese, as early as the month of June, had occupied the town of Pegu, capital of the old kingdom of that name, to the great distress of the native inhabitants, who were, however, powerless to offer resistance on their own behalf.

Pegu forms the southern portion of the Burmese Empire, and by it had been annexed in 1757. The town itself is situated some seventy miles north of Rangoon. These marauding Burmese it was now determined to dislodge, and to occupy the city by British arms. Brigadier McNeill of the Madras Army was selected by General Godwin to command the venture, but the general himself accompanied the expedition. The flotilla was commanded by Commander Shadwell.

The vessels forming the expedition dropped anchor about two miles below Pegu, which is connected by the Pegu River with the

Irrawaddy, on the evening of the 20th November. The next morning the debarkation was carried out without any opposition, the troops landing in high grass jungle, and the whole country being enveloped in a thick fog.

The position of the enemy was known to the British commander, as a previous expedition in June had enabled Captain Laller to roughly map the country. The site of the old city, which formed the enemy's position, was formed by a square surrounded by a high bund, each side of which was estimated to be two miles in length. The west side faced the river, and a moat, between 70 and 80 paces wide, ran entirely round the position. It was determined to force a way along the moat and endeavour to turn the enemy's left.

Accordingly, the advance was commenced, Captain Laller and a Burmese leading the direction of march. The Bengal Fusiliers were in front, the 5th Madras Native Infantry followed, and the Madras Fusiliers brought up the rear. The troops marched in file. Slowly and laboriously the invaders crept forward, struggling for two hours through the almost impenetrable grass and jungle along the edge of the moat, and exposed to a warm fire from the enemy. At length a part of the moat was reached which admitted a passage for the troops, but unhappily it was covered by a strong post of marksmen and two guns. From this point of vantage, the enemy kept up a galling fire, and it soon became evident the battery would have to be stormed.

Colonel Tudor, with 250 men, was ordered to drive the Burmese out, and with a cheer the gallant little band plunged into the muddy waters of the moat and, scaling the bank in front of them, drove the foe from their position with cold steel. Having mastered this point, the key of the position, Pegu did not long remain in the possession of the Burmese. With enormous difficulty, over the almost impassable ground, Captain Mallock brought forward his artillery, and kept down the enemy's fire. A short halt followed to rest the troops and collect the not inconsiderable number of wounded. A large *pagoda* now lay in the path of advance, and from this the Burmese kept up a heavy musketry fire. Here again history repeated itself. Gallantly springing forward with some 200 of the Madras and Bengal Fusiliers, the steps of the *pagoda* were soon ascended, the foe driven out, and Pegu was ours.

The amount of the Burmese force in Pegu which we drove out on capturing the town, was estimated at 4,000 or 5,000; our own troops barely amounted to 1,000 men. A garrison of 400 was left in charge, and the success of the enterprise duly reported to the governor-general at Calcutta. The immediate result was a proclamation annexing the entire province of Pegu.

Fighting, however, in the vicinity was not at an end. Day by day unceasing, but abortive, attacks were made by the Burmese to recover their lost position. Major Hill gallantly defended his post, but at length it became necessary to relieve him, and an attempt was made to bring the Burmese to a general action. Early in December, General Godwin once more left Rangoon for Pegu, and with an army of only 1,200 men proceeded to seek the enemy in his lair. After a march of a few miles through dense jungle, their position was discovered.

> They were admirably posted behind an entrenchment; large spars formed their breastwork, and it appeared to be about a mile long, filled with masses of men, a few hundreds of the Cassay horse, some elephants, and a few guns.

On the advance of the British the enemy for a time made no move beyond firing an occasional shot, and all ranks believed that at length the foe was to stand at bay. On coming, however, to close quarters, the Burmese rapidly retreated, bitterly disappointing our men, and a two days' further march in pursuit failed to bring them to a standstill, and General Godwin and his forces were compelled reluctantly to return.

No further event of importance occurred in '52, but early in the year following, taking advantage of the unsettled state of the country, and the quarrels between British and Burmese, numerous *dacoity* chiefs made inroads here and there upon the peaceful inhabitants of the country, raiding and killing and striking terror into the hearts of the country folk.

Against several of these General Godwin found it necessary to direct his forces—one in particular, a chief named Mea Toon, giving immense trouble ere he was finally subjugated. Three times was a British force led against—on two occasions on the 10th January, and again later, with disastrous results to our arms. On the second occasion he succeeded in killing as many as 50 of our men.

Finally, in March, Sir John Cleape brought the *dacoity* chief to bay, and after a severe struggle, lasting four hours, in the course of which two British officers were killed, he succeeded in overpowering the foe. The wily Mea Toon himself, however, effected his escape, and fleeing from the neighbourhood of Donnabew, where the engagement took place, escaped with his immediate following. No trouble was, however, given by him later.

The main scheme of operations now took the form of a series of attempts to bring the main Burmese Army to bay, but besides an occasional skirmish, little hard lighting resulted, the Burmese avoiding coming to grips.

Commenting on the state of the Burmese campaign at this period the *Annual Register* tersely sums up the enormous difficulties which General Godwin and the devoted troops under his command had to contend with:—

An army can do little where there are no roads, nor adequate means of transport for artillery, and when the enemy retires into jungles, and we have to contend against the heat of a tropical sun varied by long periods of incessant rain.

The end, however, was not far off. By this time the greater portion of the Burmese was under our jurisdiction, and the ultimate and final success of the British arms seemed to be but a matter of time. Such, at least, was the view taken by the King of Ava, and without the drawing un of any formal treaty he at length decided to treat for peace by granting the concessions demanded of him. Protection to British trade and life was definitely assured, and the British forces shortly thereafter withdrawn.

CHAPTER 11

The Battle of the Alma: 1854

Following upon their declarations of war with Russia, upon the 27th and 28th March, 1854, respectively, arrangements were at once made by the Governments of France and Britain for forwarding a sufficient number of troops to the East. Gallipoli, on the south side of the Sea of Marmora, was chosen as the rendezvous, and here in due course arrived the Armies of the Allies. The armies were under the respective commands of Lord Raglan and Marshal St. Arnaud. The Turkish Army, then actively engaged with the Russians upon the Ottoman frontier at Silistria, was commanded by Omar Pasha.

It was resolved by the three generals, after some preliminary disagreement by St. Arnaud, to advance the armies to Varna, in Bulgaria, and from that base to operate for the relief of Silistria, where a Turkish force was being besieged by the Russians. Our only present concern with the successful defence of Silistria (so that on June 23rd, 1854, the siege was abandoned by Russia), and with the Turkish successes upon the Lower Danube at Rustchuk, is the moral effect which they produced in Britain. At both these places the Turkish troops were practically led by young British officers who had flung themselves into the enterprise without orders, and practically for the pure love of fighting. At both these places their efforts, backed by the unflinching Turkish soldiery, had met with signal success.

The names of Butler, Nasmyth, Ballard, Bent, and others were household words in Britain. Men's eyes kindled with enthusiasm as they heard of the defeat of the dreaded armies of the *Czar* by a handful of mere boys, and now that they had, so to say, tasted blood, the people of Britain clamoured for an offensive, rather than a defensive, campaign. True, the Turkish frontier had been successfully freed from the enemy, and that without the co-operation of the Allied Armies; true, an honourable peace might be concluded with Russia at this juncture, but both these things, good enough in their way, were not satisfying.

Through the medium of the *Times* newspaper, then in its infancy, and in a hundred other ways, backed by the Minister of War, the Duke of Newcastle, and egged on by the Emperor of the French, they clamoured for the overthrow of Sebastopol. Once let that great fortress, the stronghold of the power of southern Russia, be razed to the ground, and a lasting peace might be proclaimed. But no half measures would suffice. Accordingly, the British and French Governments sent specific instructions to Lord Raglan and Marshal St. Arnaud to proceed with their armies to the Crimea, and to lay siege to the fortress of Sebastopol. This resolution and these instructions saw the commencement of the Crimean campaign.

After one or two preliminary delays, the combined fleets, with the transports containing the Allied Armies, arrived off the port of Eupatoria on the north-west coast of the Crimean Peninsula. Cholera and other forms of sickness, which had been rife amongst the armies during their stay at Varna, showed little abatement on the voyage, as had been hoped, and many men fell victims to the dread disease. It was found that the port of Eupatoria was undefended, but its formal surrender was demanded, in connection with which formality an amusing incident arose. The governor of the place, having an unfailing respect for his own official position, and regarding the formalities of the health regulations of Eupatoria as of paramount importance, calmly, in the face of the Allied Armies and fleets, insisted upon fumigating and disinfecting the "summons to surrender" in accordance with the government health regulations! Moreover, he informed the representatives of the Powers that persons landing would have to consider themselves in quarantine for the prescribed period!

From the few Tartar inhabitants of Eupatoria the allies were able to buy cattle and forage, a matter of vital importance to the armies, and after its formal surrender on the 13th September, 1854, the fleet proceeded southward along the coast, anchoring off the Old Fort in Kalamita Bay. The British force landed at the south of the Lake of Kamishlee, and the French slightly to the south of them. By the 18th all were landed, the British numbering 27,000, including 1,000 cavalry and 60 guns; Turks about 7,000 infantry; and the French 30,000 infantry, with 68 guns.

Partially overcoming the difficulties of land transport by the capture, by Sir Richard Airey, the quartermaster-general, of a stray Cossack convoy (some 350 waggons were obtained), the Allied Armies

The Battle of the Alma

were to move south upon Sebastopol. It was decided they should march parallel with the coast, escorted by their fleets on their right flank. On the morning of the 19th September the march began. The British Army took the left, the French and Turks the centre, and the fleets formed the right of the advance.

Between the allies and Sebastopol flow several rivers, from the high levels of the Crimea to the sea, at right angles to the line of march. The first of these is the Bulganak, the second the Alma.

On the march the troops suffered severely from thirst and cholera; many men fell out from weakness also, but by evening the River Bulganak was readied, and a force sent back to bring in the stragglers.

At the Bulganak the first sight of the enemy, in any force, was obtained, in the shape of a body of cavalry some 2,000 strong, backed by 6,000 infantry with two batteries. The enemy were observing the advance of the allies from the opposite hill on the far side of the river. For our advance guard of four squadrons of cavalry, in marching order, to engage so large a force in position would have been folly. Accordingly, Lord Raglan gave orders for our cavalry to withdraw—a movement which was promptly followed by the Russian artillery fire. Several horses were killed and two men wounded, but the manoeuvre was effected successfully, and by the time it was accomplished our main support were in sight. The enemy accordingly disappeared, with the loss of 35 cavalrymen killed or wounded by our artillery, now by this time brought into action.

This was the first combat of any importance in the Crimean campaign, and at its conclusion our troops received orders to bivouac on the banks of the river. Owing to the proximity of the enemy, and fearing an attack at dawn, Lord Raglan gave the command to bivouac in order of battle. He himself passed the night in a posthouse by the riverside.

In the morning, however, the enemy was nowhere to be seen, and it was subsequently ascertained that he had fallen back to his entrenched position on the far side of the Alma. Early in the morning of the 20th September, 1854, the Allied Armies left their position by the Bulganak and marched forward towards the Alma. The order maintained was, in the main, similar to that of the previous day. The fleet defended the right, the French and Turks marched in the centre, and the British took the left.

Now the Russian position on the far side of the Alma was a strong one. Though the ground to the north of the river slopes down gently to the riverside, and is covered by gardens and vineyards, on the south of the river hills rise to a considerable height almost from the water's edge. This range of hills formed the Russian position.

Nearest to the sea is a hill with steep sides, so steep that the Russian commander-in-chief, Prince Mentschikoff, the former ambassador to Constantinople, deemed it impossible for any troops to scale them. This hill is called the West Cliff. Joined on to it, and forming as it were an eastern shoulder, is the Telegraph Height, so called from the fact that at the time of the battle a telegraph line was in course of construction upon its summit. East of this again is a valley through which runs the main road to Sebastopol, flanked on the other side by the Kourgané Hill. East of this again the ground slopes away more gently.

Deeming the Western Cliff inaccessible, the Russian commander had not thought fit to defend it, but upon the ledge which intervened between the river and the Telegraph Height he posted four militia battalions, with four battalions of regular infantry as supports, and four battalions of the Moscow corps, a few companies of the 6th Rifles, and a ten-gun battery—the whole under the command of General Kiviakoff. These troops faced the French Army. In the pass between the Telegraph Height and the Kourgané Hill, and opposite the British second division, were posted four battalions of light infantry, the Borodino corps, some 6th Rifles, and a battalion of sappers near the bridge crossing the Alma.

Across the main road were 16 guns (later called the Causeway battery), with eight other guns to the east of them. These forces, constituting the Russian centre, were commanded by Prince Gortschakoff. The Russian right, on the Kourgané Hill, which at the commencement of the battle faced our Light Division (and later, the Guards and Highlanders) consisted of 16 battalions of infantry, 2 battalions of sailors, 12 heavy guns in the fortified embrasure of the Great Redoubt, and 4 batteries of field artillery, one of which formed the Lesser Redoubt; General Koetzinski commanded. In addition to these troops, the Russian cavalry consisted of 16 squadrons, with 11 *sotnias* of Cossacks. Altogether 39,000 troops, including 3,600 horsemen and 96 guns.

The allied troops were disposed as follows. On the extreme right, next to the sea-coast, were the brigades of Generals Bouat and Autemarre, under the chief command of General Bosquet, and supported by the majority of the Turks. On the left of these, but far in their rear, marched the 7th Division under Camobert, and the 3rd under Prince Napoleon, moving abreast and supported by the 4th Division under Forey, with the remaining Turks. On the left of these again came the British 2nd Division, under Sir de Lacy Evans, supported by the 3rd (Sir Richard England). On the left of Evans again, the Light Division, under Sir George Brown, preceded by the 2nd Rifle Battalion of skirmishers, and supported by the 1st Division under the Duke of Cambridge, parallel with whom moved the 4th Division under Sir George Cathcart, The Earl of Lucan commanded the cavalry. The constitution of the British Divisions was as follows:—

1st. Division—Grenadiers, Coldstreams, Scots Fusiliers, with the Black Watch, Camerons, and Sutherland Highlanders; 2nd Division—30th, 55th, 41st, 47th and 49th regiments; 3rd Division—38th, 50th, 1st Royal Scots, 4th, 44th, 28th and 63rd regiments; 4th Division—20th, 21st, 63rd, 57th, with 1st Battalion Rifles and cavalry.

Briefly, the plan of attack was this—the French and Turks were first to turn the enemy's left, then the British were to attack him in front, Advancing in the warm sunshine in the order above indicated, the allies made a final halt before the battle at about a mile and a half from the river, on the ground which slopes gently down to the north bank. From this point the enemy's position could be more or less clearly seen, a deep scar upon the slopes of the Kourgané Hill showing the position of the Great Redoubt.

It was at this time that there occurred, as Kinglake tells us, that "singular pause of sound," when a sudden stillness fell upon the Allied Armies, so intense that the slightest noise could be heard over the field for a long distance. It seemed, indeed, that fighting was the occurrence least of all to be expected an idea quickly dispelled by the veteran Sir Colin Campbell, who remarked that the opportunity would be a good one "for the men to get loose half their cartridges."

During the carrying out of this order, the two commanders, Lord Raglan and St. Arnaud, rode forward entirely alone to reconnoitre the enemy's position with their field glasses. As the marshal neared our lines, he was cheered by the British soldiers, and, raising his hat, he replied in excellent English, "Hurrah for old England!"

By this time, one o'clock arrived, and the general advance was sounded. At twenty-five minutes past' one, the allied fleets opened fire upon the Telegraph Height, and the infantry massed upon the ledge at its base. The result of this fire was that the Russian troops at this place, under General Kiviakoff, withdrew further up the hill towards the Telegraph.

At 1.30 the Russians opened fire. Accounts vary as to the first man hit. Some say he was a drummer carrying a letter, and that he was positively broken in two by a round shot. Others have it that it was an artilleryman riding in front of his gun: but, be this as it may, at length battle was engaged between the land forces. From this point onward the enemy's artillery fire was brisk, and soon afterwards the 1st Division came into range, and was accordingly thrown into line, and the men lay down.

Lord Raglan and his staff were at this point objects of attention to the enemy's artillery, a heavy fire being directed at the brilliant uniforms of the headquarters staff as they moved about the field from place to place.

Now, as before stated, Bosquet faced the West Cliff, Camobert the west side of the Telegraph Height, Prince Napoleon was opposite the Telegraph Height, and Evans, the village of Bourliouk. On his left was Sir George Brown. Suddenly the village of Bourliouk was set on fire, no one knows how, and the immediate result was a contraction of the British front in order to avoid the stifling smoke and heat, such a contraction threatening to be of considerable advantage to the enemy.

Meanwhile, Bosquet's operations for turning the Russian left had been pushed forward, and were taking effect. His troops, in two divisions, crossed the river respectively at its bar and at the village of Almatamack shortly after two o'clock, and began to ascend the steep West Cliff, encountering no enemy. On gaining the summit, however, they were received by a tremendous fire from the Russian battery No. 4, and for a few seconds thrown into confusion. Almost identically, however, the French artillery arrived and supported Bosquet's force effectively, with the result that their twelve pieces silenced no fewer than forty of the enemy's guns.

Meantime the Russian commander, Prince Mentschikoff, hearing of the attack on his left, moved four batteries, seven battalions of foot, and four squadrons of hussars towards the threatened point, but ere they reached it he seems to have changed his mind, and ordered a counter-march, thereby rendering this large body of troops entirely useless at a critical period of the fight. Bosquet was accordingly allowed to retain the West Cliff, which he had won, but was almost entirely unsupported, and in considerable danger.

Accordingly, St. Arnaud ordered Generals Camobert and Prince Napoleon to advance, in words which the great historian of the war has recorded:—

With men such as you I have no orders to give; I have but to point to the enemy.

The advance commenced, and was not wanting in incident. At one time Prince Napoleon was in great danger. General Thomas, perceiving a ball coming in the direction of the prince, cried to him, "Take care!" and the prince, putting spurs to his horse, avoided it with the utmost coolness. It, however, struck M. Leblanc, the military intendant, with the result that his leg had to be amputated.

Now, had the advance of these two divisions been successfully carried out, there seems little doubt that the subsequent scheme of battle would have been considerably altered. For two reasons, however, the French divisions halted when they had crossed the river and were about to scale the opposite steeps. The first was that the ground on the far side was found to be too steep for artillery, and the maxims of the French Army forbade infantry from advancing unsupported under such circumstances. Accordingly, the guns had to be sent round by the ford at the village of Almatamack, causing inevitable delay.

The second cause was the unfortunate panic which set in, not unnaturally, amongst the rear ranks of the divisions owing to the galling fire to which they were exposed. The front ranks, being under shelter of the steep river banks, were, more or less, halted in safety, but the rear ranks were directly exposed to the Russian batteries posted on the Great Road. The measures taken to rectify this state of affairs unfortunately only served to aggravate it. Part of the 4th Division was sent to support Camobert, and this, by increasing the mass of men exposed to fire, naturally increased the slaughter which at this stage has been described as almost a massacre.

At this time the Russians might have materially altered the aspect of affairs by taking advantage of Bosquet's isolated position, and by a free use of the cavalry at their disposal. But neither of these steps were taken.

To Lord Raglan was communicated the state of affairs on the French side of the battle. Immediate action must be taken if Bosquet's successful advance was not to be nullified. For an hour and a half our troops had been under the enemy's fire, and had suffered heavily. This circumstance, together with the repeated requests of the French *aides-de-camp*, determined Lord Raglan, at the risk of spoiling the symmetry of his front and of the original plan of advance, to move forward at once.

Those present have recorded the joy of all ranks when the order flew down the lines like magic. Nolan it was, of the 15th Hussars, who afterwards carried the fatal order that was to decimate the Light Brigade at Balaclava, who now bore the command down the cheering ranks, and in a few moments the whole of the foremost British line advanced in order towards the river. A few momenta later still and Nolan had a horse shot under him as he rode forward with the advance brigade.

Owing to the burning village of Bourliouk, Sir de Lacy Evans, commanding the 2nd Division, had to cut his force into two parts, one passing on the right and the other on the left of the conflagration. The Russian fire from the Causeway batteries was heavy. Evans himself was struck, and nearly all his staff wounded, and some indeed killed. On the left moved forward the Light Division under Sir George Brown, opposed to whom were the Great Redoubt and no fewer than eighteen battalions of infantry, including the famous Kayan battalion.

Straight down through the vineyards and across the river, somehow or other, moved the Light Division. The orders were not to halt until the river had been crossed. It has been reported that some few men, fearing the hail of bullets, which, by reason of their sound among the foliage, seemed in the vineyards to be nearly doubled, took refuge in the farmhouses which stood here and there. But such men were very few, and soon the whole division, under Generals Buller and Codrington, stood on the Russian side of the Alma, sheltered for a moment by the steep river bank. Here Buller, on the extreme left, halted and reformed his men, holding back the 88th and 77th regiments to protect the Allied Army from a flank attack.

The remaining five battalions of the Light Brigade pressed forward up the bank, and Sir George Brown himself it was, on horseback, flushed and breathless, who first gained the summit, a mark for the entire Russian artillery. That he remained unshot was a miracle. Simultaneously, Codrington and the Royal Fusiliers, under Lacy Yea, gained the summit of the river bank, and the five battalions pressed on up the hill.

Facing them, on their right and left, wore the Kayan infantry columns; in the centre was the Great Redoubt. The Kayan columns on the British left were soon put to flight by the Riflemen, the 19th, and the Royal Welsh, who had joined the centre for the attack upon the Great Redoubt, but the Kayan column on the right engaged the Royal Fusiliers in a stubborn fight.

Terrible was the death roll as our Light Division pressed up the hill towards the Great Redoubt. Men fell on every side. The Welsh and Royal Fusiliers suffered heavily, and for a moment had to pause and reform. The gallant colonel of the Welsh Fusiliers was killed in the front of his men, and with the words "On, lads, on!" upon his lips. Old Sir George Brown was knocked from his horse, but rose immediately, and remounted with the assistance of a rifleman named Hannan, who coolly asked, "Are your stirrups the right length, sir?" Up swept the scarlet coats, only pausing for a second now and again to reform.

During one of these pauses the Eddingtons were killed. The two brothers were in the 95th, the Derbyshires. Captain Eddington was deliberately murdered by a Russian rifleman when lying wounded on the field, when his brother, perceiving the act, rushed forward, in a frenzy, in advance of the regiment to avenge him, and fell, literally torn to pieces by a storm of grape shot. But the men pressed on in spite of all the carnage around them, and then suddenly, as they neared the Redoubt, the smoke lifted for a moment, and disclosed the Russian gunners limbering up and making off.

Quick as lightning, young Ensign Anstruther of the Royal Welsh rushed forward with the colours of the regiment, and, outstripping all, succeeded in planting them upon the parapet of the Redoubt. A second later and he fell back riddled with shot, dragging the colours involuntarily with him. A sergeant of the same regiment, Luke O'Connor, seized the colours again, and planted them firmly upon the wall of the Redoubt, when General Codrington, uncovering, saluted the colours, and leapt his horse into the embrasure just as the last of the enemy's guns galloped off. In the fight no fewer than thirty-one officers and non-commissioned officers had been killed. One Russian gun was captured in the act of withdrawing.

By this time the 1st Division under the Duke of Cambridge, consisting of the Guards and Highlanders, was moving to the support of the Light Division, who thus occupied the Great Redoubt. But as yet they were only at the river, so the Light Division found themselves isolated, while before them were the Vladimir regiment, supported by the Ouglity corps and others, sixteen battalions in all with horse and artillery.

In the meantime, the position of affairs on the allied right, where Camobert and Prince Napoleon's divisions were advancing to the support of Bosquet, was distinctly unpromising for the allies. The heavy column under Kiviakoff had checked Camobert's advance, and

Prince Napoleon was not yet in touch with the enemy.

At this juncture there happened that which is perhaps unique in the history of battles. On the one side a large proportion of the Russian army was engaged with the French attack, on the other their troops were about to push the British down from the ground which they had so hardly won in the storming of the Great Redoubt. In the centre, however, to the Russian left of the Causeway batteries, there were in the meantime no troops, and here Lord Raglan found himself in his eager pushing forward to obtain a clear view of all that was happening.

The effect of the appearance of Lord Raglan and his staff upon the rising ground in the centre was tremendous. The Russian right, on the Kourgané Hill, seeing a group of staff officers in the centre of the Russian lines, supposed that the French had been entirely successful in their part of the field, and accordingly halted to take counsel as they were in the act of advancing upon our unsupported troops who had won, and were now occupying, the Great Redoubt.

Not content, however, with the moral effect of his presence, the significance of which he fully appreciated, Lord Raglan ordered a couple of nine-pounder guns to be brought up to him, and with these (Colonel Dickson working one of the guns with his own hands, says Kinglake), he opened fire upon the flank of the Causeway batteries, and upon the enemy's reserves. The Causeway batteries retreated higher up the road, leaving it open for Evans' advance; the enemy's reserves were disorganised, and the Russian right advance was for the moment paralysed.

General Evans was quick to seize the opportunity. Advancing up the road with his troops, and with the batteries of Sir Richard England, directed by that general in person, he drove back the Russian artillery and took up a firm stand in line with Lacy Yea and his Royal Fusiliers, who, it will be remembered, were still engaged with the (Russian) left Kayan battalion. The fight here was a stubborn one, and much depended upon it, for as long as the fusiliers could hold their own, and keep the Kayan battalion fully occupied, our troops to their right could take up an effective position with comparative ease.

But the fusiliers did more. Assisted by the 55th Regiment, who had been gradually advancing up the hill, and who now poured a flanking fire into the Russians, they routed the Kayan battalion. This advantage was followed up by the Guards, who passing the severely battered but victorious fusiliers, led the van of that second severe fight on the Kourgané Hill, which ultimately terminated in victory for the

Allied Armies.

Seen at this point of the battle, the British line was more or less continuous, and was formed as follows, from its right the Grenadiers, covering the Fusiliers reforming; the Coldstreams, the Black Watch, Camerons and Sutherland Highlanders in the order named. Opposed to them were the Vladimir columns, supported as before on either hand by the Kayan columns, that on the British right sadly disorganised by its sanguinary encounter with the Royal Fusiliers.

It was a battle of column against line, the Russians being commanded by Prince Gortshakoff in person, under whom was the brave General Koetzinski.

The fight did not last long. Deceived by the apparent numbers of the red-coated troops advancing in line; assailed with ferocity by the redoubtable Black Watch under Sir Colin Campbell, whose command of "Forward, 42nd!" has become world-renowned; now stormed by the impetuous 93rd, in the main composed of men whose eagerness to fight had led them to exchange into it rather than be left at home; at length roughly handled by the 75th, and unsettled by the successful operations of the allies on their left, where the Causeway batteries were in retreat the powerful columns broke up after a short but stubborn fight, in which, many fell on both sides, and beat an angry and reluctant retreat from the field of battle. Deepthroated sobs of rage were heard as the great grey-coated columns drew off, and to the last, General Koetzinski, borne wounded in a litter, directed the operations of the retreat from the very rear of his defeated army.

So, one after another, Vladimir, Kayan, Sousdal, and lastly the reserve columns were driven from the field with slaughter and harried by our horse artillery so that, in places, the killed and wounded "formed small heaps and banks." Of the four Russian generals in this part of the field, three were wounded. The loss of the Kayan battalion alone is estimated at 1,700. The loss of the Guards and Highlanders together was no more than 500 men.

Meantime in the French part of the field, General Camobert's artillery had crossed the Alma at Almatamack, and now, returning eastwards along the Russian bank of the river, were engaged in shelling Kiviakoff's battalions on the Telegraph Height. Bosquet's artillery fire was also directed upon these troops, and General Kiviakoff supposed the fire to be coming from the ships of the allied fleets. Seeing, in addition to these calamities (for the execution done by the French guns was considerable), the turn of the tide on the Russian right of the field, General Kiviakoff ordered a retreat, and shortly the Telegraph Heights were occupied by the warlike *Zouaves*.

A few Russian riflemen, who had for some reason failed to move, were overwhelmed by the bayonet, and, in spite of a heavy fire from Kiviakoff's retreating battalions, the standard of the 39th French regiment was planted on the Telegraph Height. Lieutenant Portevin was killed by a cannon ball in the act of hoisting it, and later, Marshal St. Arnaud in person thanked the *Zouaves* on the summit of the hill.

After traversing a couple of miles, Kiviakoff succeeded in halting his men and in once more facing the French fire, but panic soon set in, and a confused rabble of men, guns, and horses trailed off towards the River Katcha.

In no part of the field was the retreat followed up to any extent; our men were for the most part wearied, and our cavalry arm was weak, while Marshal St. Arnaud found it "impossible" for the French Army to advance further that day. Had these things been otherwise, there is every probability that much of the later campaign might have been curtailed, if not indeed rendered unnecessary.

As Lord Raglan rode along the field after the fight, loud British cheers arose from regiment to regiment, now slowly reforming, till, says Kinglake:—

> From the spurs of the Telegraph Height to the easternmost bounds of the crest which had been won by the Highland Brigade, those desolate hills in Crimean Tartary were made to sound like England.

But in spite of this, Lord Raglan was sad and thoughtful, and spent many hours among the sheds and farmhouses where lay the wounded. In the evening he dined with only two others in a small marquee beside the Alma.

The allies camped where they found themselves at the termination of the fight. The total of French losses, killed and wounded, was between 500 and 600, though a much higher figure was supplied in the preliminary official returns. The British lost a total of 2,002 of all ranks, and the Russians no fewer than 5,709, including 5 generals and 193 other officers. On the morning of the 21st September, the dead were buried, and a huge mound some five hundred yards from the river marks their last resting place. Many lives might have been saved had not the number of surgeons and appliances been wholly inadequate. On the 22nd, the Allied Armies resumed their march.

CHAPTER 12

The Battle of Balaclava: 1854

Early on the morning of the 23rd September, 1854, the Allied Armies left their camp on the battlefield of Alma, and marched northwards towards Sebastopol. Traces of the haste in which the Russian Army had retreated were at hand on every side. Here a sword, there a pistol, a belt, or even a tunic; the broad track, strewn with such relics, showed clearly the path of the retreat.

At length the valley of the Katcha was reached, and the camp pitched for the night. The advance was resumed early next morning, and about mid-day, from the ridge of hills separating the valley of the Katcha from that of the Baltic, the armies looked down upon their goal, Sebastopol.

During a brief halt, Marshal St. Arnaud, whose bodily weakness was increasing day by day, dismounted and lay upon the ground. Men noticed that he looked sad and worn. He was, in fact, within a few days of his death.

Here a council of war was held, and it was determined that the northern side of Sebastopol was too strong to admit of an immediate assault, and finally the decision was arrived at of executing a flank march inland and attacking Sebastopol from the south. By the 26th September this somewhat perilous movement was carried out with success, and the little seaport of Balaclava surrendered to Lord Raglan without bloodshed. On the same night, Marshal St. Arnaud resigned his command to General Camobert, and three days later he died on board ship, whither he had been carried for passage to France.

Balaclava was of vast importance to the allies, as its tiny harbour gave them a means of communication with their fleets whilst these were still out of the range of the guns of Sebastopol. Accordingly, the place was garrisoned by troops under Sir Colin Campbell, whilst the main army moved northward a few miles to within a convenient distance of Sebastopol, where they spent many days, some twenty in all, disposing their forces, erecting batteries, and making all the necessary preparations for a prolonged and persistent siege.

Meanwhile, the Russians busily fortified the place, glad of the unexpected delay, since they had anticipated an immediate assault. Several of the finest ships were sunk at the mouth of the harbour to keep the allied fleets at bay, and works of counter-fortification went busily forward. Admiral Korniloff and Colonel Todleben were the two chief officers in command, Prince Mentschikoff having withdrawn the main portion of his army to the Baltic, where he remained for a considerable period in a state of extraordinary inactivity. By the 6th October, however, he was prevailed upon to increase the garrison of Sebastopol to some 53,000 men.

On the 17th October, 1854, the Allied Armies opened fire upon Sebastopol, and the deafening cannonade was maintained daily till the evening of the 25th October. An account of the siege and final surrender of Sebastopol is given, in a later chapter.

In the meantime, on the 18th October, a Russian field army was observed to be manoeuvring on the allied flank and rear, and threatening the somewhat isolated garrison of Balaclava. The defensive measures taken for the defence of Balaclava consisted of inner and outer lines of defence. The town and harbour themselves were protected by steep hills, except at the gorge of Kadikoi, towards the north. Accordingly, these hills were fortified by the marine artillery, and held by marines and two companies of the 93rd regiment, while the gorge of Kadikoi itself was defended by six companies of the 93rd Highlanders and a battalion of Turks, with artillery, the whole constituting the inner line of defence.

Now the gorge of Kadikoi opens out into a more or less level plain known as the plain of Balaclava, a mile north of the town. It was here that there was destined to be fought the great, cavalry battle which holds so glorious a place in annals of the British Army. Right across the centre of this plain, which is three miles long by two broad, and hemmed in on all sides by hills from 300 to 400 feet high, is a low continuous chain of hills or ridge dividing the plain of Balaclava into two portions, called respectively the north and south valleys, and carrying the main Woronzoff Road or Causeway.

This ridge of hills was known to our men as the Causeway heights, and constituted the outer line of defence, by which the enemy might be hindered from even penetrating to the south valley. A chain of

BATTLE OF BALACLAVA

redoubts were thrown up along the Causeway heights by our engineers and manned by Turks. The only supporting force available in the event of an attack was the cavalry, under Lord Lucan, some 1,500 strong, which was encamped in the south valley within the outer line of defence.

The cavalry force consisted of two brigades—the Heavy Brigade, composed of the Scots Greys, Enniskillens, 1st. Royal Dragoons, and 4th and 5th Dragoon Guards, under General Hon. James Scarlett, and the Light Brigade, under Lord Cardigan, consisting of the 4th and 13th Light Dragoons, the 8th and 11th Hussars, and the 17th Lancers. The whole garrison of Balaclava was, as before mentioned, under the chief command of Sir Colin Campbell.

On the evening of the 24th October, the troops of all divisions turned in for the night as usual, little conscious of the fact that a force of 25,000 Russians was advancing stealthily towards them from three different directions, their object being to seize the outer line of defence. Arising an hour before daybreak, Lord Lucan and his staff, mounted and moving slowly along in an easterly direction, perceived, in the dim light, two ensigns flying from the easternmost redoubt! Instantly all was activity, for the flying of two ensigns from the fort was the signal prearranged with the Turks to announce the Russian advance in force. The Light Cavalry Brigade was sent forward to support the Turks, and an *aide-de-camp* was despatched at full speed to Lord Raglan informing him at once of the turn of affairs.

A private soldier of the Black Watch says:—

> It so happened that all our regiment was in camp, and we were expecting to get that day's rest, but the rations were scarcely served out when the words came, 'Fall in! fall in at once!' I need not say that the order was obeyed in, all haste by the whole division, and His Royal Highness (The Duke of Cambridge) and Colonel Cameron marched us off in the direction of Balaclava.

Thus the 1st and 4th Divisions with Bosquet's forces were promptly despatched to the scene of action, but meantime, in the plain of Balaclava things were happening.

The Turkish defence had not lasted long. Contrary to popular opinion, the historian of the war extols the bravery of the Turkish troops at this juncture, who, if they were compelled to beat an ignominious retreat, did so at least in the presence of overwhelming numbers of the enemy, and practically without support from our troops. In a very little while the outer line of defence was captured, the Russian cavalry in the meantime proceeding down the north valley towards the gorge of Kadikoi. Here, it will be remembered, Sir Colin Campbell stood awaiting them in person with the 93rd Highlanders.

As the foremost Russian horsemen appeared heading towards the gorge, the eager Highlanders began to spring forward, but; the angry voice of their veteran commander held them in check, and saved them from being cut to pieces by the cavalry in the open plain. Meanwhile the Turkish fugitives streaming down the south valley towards Kadikoi, had been formed up into some sort of order by Sir Colin, and together with the 93rd they stood awaiting the Russian cavalry charge. That charge never came. But while the steady line of Highlanders poured a heavy fire into the advancing force, without waiting for its effect, the Osmaulis turned and fled, falling over each other in their haste. The Highlanders alone confronted the foe.

"Remember, there is no retreat, men!" said Sir Colin, as he rode along the line; "you must die where you stand!"

"Ay, ay, Sir Colin," came the quick reply, and a second later the order rang out clear and sharp, and a second heavy volley met the advancing enemy.

It proved too much for the dreaded horsemen of the *Czar*, and in a few moments, they turned and retreated in confusion, another volley helping them on their way. The strain relaxed, the victorious Highlanders turned their faces to watch the retreating soldiers of the *sultan*, and in a moment, where had been set, stern faces and lips drawn tight, were seen countenances convulsed with laughter and powder-stained cheeks furrowed by tears of uncontrollable merriment.

For in their retreat past the camp of the Highlanders some of the Turkish soldiers had paused for a second with intent, it is supposed, to pillage. Judge then of their amazement when from out of one of the nearest tents emerged a stalwart and furious Scottish "wife," who seized the nearest of the Faithful by the ear and with stout stick and sturdy arm belaboured his back and his red trousers till the blows resounded far and wide. Not once, but again and again did this angry lady ("she was a very powerful woman," said an eye-witness) belabour the soldiers of the *sultan*, and long and loud was the laughter of the 93rd as Turk after Turk fled screaming from her fury, bawling, "Ship! ship!" as he sought a safer refuge at the harbour of Balaclava. Kinglake says:—

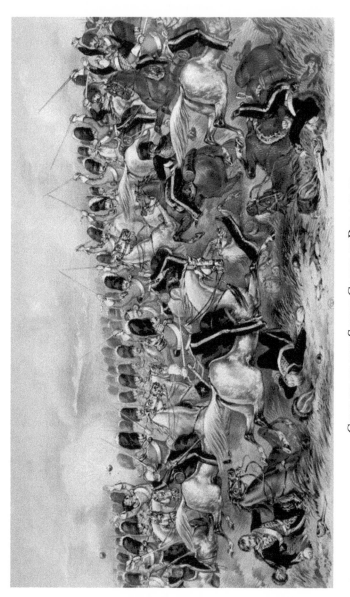

Charge of the Scots Greys at Balaclava

Then, if ever in history, did the fortunes of Islam wane low before the manifest ascendant of the Cross!

In the meantime, in the other part of the field events moved quickly. The defeated squadron of Russian Horse rejoined the main body in the north valley, and under General Ryjoff moved up to the crest of the Causeway heights, between the captured redoubts, with the intention of falling upon our troops in the south valley. By this time Lord Raglan had arrived upon the scene, and from a position where he could view the whole field observed the Turkish flight at Kadikoi. Quick as thought he directed the Heavy Brigade under General Scarlett to proceed to their support. As the brigade rode along the south valley in execution of this order, they were suddenly aware of a squadron of Russian cavalry gazing down upon them from the Causeway heights upon their left, and about to hurl itself upon their flank.

To face about was the work of an instant, though the odds were about ten to one, and for a few seconds our cavalry awaited the Russian charge. At a well-governed speed and in splendid order the Russians rode down the slopes of the hill, gradually gathering impetus to press the charge, when, from some unexplained cause, their trumpets sounded, the pace gradually slackened, and the whole squadron came to a standstill within some four hundred yards of our troops, and slowly opened out their front as if to envelope our forces.

Scarlett was quick to seize this advantage accorded to him as if by a miracle. Turning to his trumpeter, he called out, "Sound the charge!" and in an instant, with their gallant general several paces in advance, the Heavy Brigade hurled themselves up the hill straight at the halted Russian line.

The front of our "three hundred" was composed of the Scots Greys and Enniskillens, regiments long associated with each other in battle, and old comrades in arms. Side by side they dashed up the gently-sloping ground, and "the Greys with a low eager moan of outbursting desire, the Enniskillens with a cheer," met the enemy with a terrific shock.

Well was it for the gallant General Scarlett that he had ridden several paces in advance of his men, and, hacking and hewing his way single-handed, had cut deeply into the mass of Russian horsemen. For their very numbers became a source of safety instead of danger to him, so that he was enabled completely to escape the shock of the charge of his own devoted troops, which completely crushed the first

111

few ranks of the Russians. After the first fierce shock, the fighting became individual. Here a single scarlet horseman engaged with three or four of the enemy, preserving his life solely by the strength of his sword-arm. There a little knot of three or four cut a pathway through overwhelming odds. One of the Scots Greys after the fight wrote:—

> I never felt less fear in my life, I felt more like a devil than a man, I escaped without a scratch, though I was covered with blood.

General Scarlett himself received five wounds, none of which was he conscious of at the time, while Lieutenant Elliot, his *aide-de-camp*, had no fewer than fourteen sabre cuts, through which he not only lived, but lived to be returned as "slightly wounded"!

The Russians suffered heavily, as our frenzied men cut their way through and through their overwhelming mass. Spectators have described the awe with which they watched this devoted body of scarlet-clad men merge themselves into the sea of Russian grey, and many thought they must be lost indeed. But the keen and practised eye of the commander-in-chief saw that, far from being overwhelmed, our men, though scattered, were more than holding their own. It was indeed the first step to victory if it could be pushed home without delay. The joy with which the order to support "the three hundred" was received may be well judged from the spirit of Lord Cardigan, who, with the soon to be famous Light Brigade, was halted watching the combat, and eagerly awaiting the order to "go in."

"Damn those Heavies!" cried the earl many times, as in sheer rage at the enforced inaction, he cantered furiously up and down the lines of his squadron; "Damn those Heavies: they'll have the laugh of us this day!" A spirit shared, it may be stated, by every British trooper on the scene. But it was not to the Light Brigade that Lord Raglan sent the order "to support," but to the comrades of the three hundred—the Heavy Dragoons and Royals.

With wild cheers, and a charge which developed in many places into a neck-and-neck race, these drove in upon the flanks of the Russian horse, and beset the sorely-pressed Cossacks at many different points. Till at length attacked both from within, where the acting-adjutant of the Greys, Alexander Miller, towering on his enormous horse and holding aloft his reeking sword, was collecting his regiment with a stentorian, "Rally, the Greys!"—attacked from without by the Royals and dragoons, and again charged from within by the Enniskillens—the Russian horsemen began to back, their ranks loosened, and soon they galloped up the hill for dear life in full retreat.

Then, as our Heavy Brigade, slowly and laboriously reformed, there went up such a cheer from the 93rd and all who had witnessed the fight as could be heard afar and all across the plain. A French general exclaimed generously, "The victory of the Heavy Brigade was the finest thing I ever saw." Sir Colin Campbell, galloping up to where the Greys were reforming, uncovered and spoke to the regiment.

"Greys! gallant Greys!" he said, according to one version, "I am sixty-one years old, and if I were young again, I should be proud to be in your ranks." Nor was this all. As General Scarlett, bloodstained from head to foot, having cut his way from one end of the Russian cavalry to the other, emerged upon the scene, an *aide-de-camp* tore up to him from Lord Raglan, and nearly throwing his horse upon its haunches, with hand at the salute, delivered in the ears of the regiment the chief's gracious message of "Well done!" which caused the hearts of all to swell with pride and eyes to gleam with joy.

But Lord Raglan was not the man to waste precious time, and instantly comprehending that now at once was the occasion to push home the cavalry victory, sent two successive orders to Sir George Cathcart, whose 4th Division was by this time approaching the scene, to at once press on and recapture the redoubts. These orders for some reason were somewhat sluggishly obeyed, and so great was the delay that Lord Raglan, growing impatient, determined to use his swifter cavalry arm.

An *aide-de-camp* with written instructions was despatched post haste to Lord Lucan, to order that the cavalry should advance and recover the heights. Here again the order was misunderstood, Lord Lucan being indisposed to move too far forward without supports, and a delay of half an hour occurred.

Minute after minute passed by as Lord Raglan and his staff from the higher ground swept the field with their glasses, and still no cavalry appeared. Then all at once it was perceived that the enemy with ropes and horses, was preparing to drag off the captured British guns.

Instantly Lord Raglan despatched the world-renowned "fourth order," the text of which was clear and unmistakable. It ran as follows:—

Lord Raglan wishes the cavalry to advance rapidly to the front, and try to prevent the enemy carrying away the guns. Troops of horse artillery may accompany. French cavalry is on your left.

Immediate.

To Captain Nolan—"the impetuous Nolan"—was entrusted the carrying of this message, and many have recorded the dangerous and breakneck speed at which he set off upon his errand, riding straight down the steep face of the hill, turning his horse's head neither to right nor left, on his urgent journey to Lord Lucan. As one who had been with Lord Raglan watching and waiting for the appearance of the cavalry who never came, it may be readily imagined that Nolan was in a temper, and briefly and uncompromisingly he thrust the order into the hands of his superior officer.

Once again Lord Lucan conceived the enterprise a dangerous one, and ventured unwisely to say so. Nolan, by this time thoroughly roused, blurted out, "Lord Raglan's orders are that the cavalry should advance immediately," and, says Lord Lucan in his narrative, pointed to the north valley, where the Russian guns were dimly seen in battery. It is probable, nay, almost certain, that Nolan merely waved his hand in a general forward direction, but Lord Lucan conceived him to indicate, the north valley.

Stung by the implied reproach of his inferior, Lord Lucan resolved to carry out the order at once, as he conceived it, and straightway commanded Lord Cardigan that the cavalry were to advance, not, as Lord Raglan had intended, up the Causeway heights, to recapture our own lost guns, but up the deadly north valley, where the enemy's guns were in position on every side.

Well did the Earl of Cardigan know the awful danger of the task thus erroneously allotted to him, but to Lord Lucan's order he returned a cheerful "Certainly sir!" and, placing himself at the head of hi men, quietly gave the order, "The brigade will advance!"

Again, and again poets and historians have placed on record the fearless devotion to duty thus called into play, and if the advance of the Light Brigade was one of the gravest military errors ever made, yet its achievement forms one of the noblest pages of the national military history.

"Gallop!" came the order, short and sharp, and as one man the 673 of all ranks bent to the saddle, and, with Lord Cardigan at their head, swept over the grassy sward straight to where the Russian guns stood, backed by five and twenty thousand horse and foot.

For a moment the foe were paralysed at the awe-inspiring folly of the British. They gasped to see the small body of cavalry, with faces set, their chargers with manes and tails streaming in the wind, galloping down the deadly valley to their death. Then their wonder gave place to rage. From right and left and straight in front burst forth a sheet of flame, and with a deafening crash the hail of lead tore through the devoted ranks.

One of the first to fall was Nolan, who had joined the charge, a volunteer, and right in front of the division rode with uplifted sword, to the intense fury of Lord Cardigan, who claimed that proud position for himself. There is little doubt that Nolan intended to change the direction of the charge, seeing at last the full extent of the error which had been made, but this was not to be. A fragment of a Russian shell tore Nolan's gallant breast. Kinglake says:—

And from what had been Nolan there burst forth a cry so strange and so appalling that the hussar who rode nearest him has always called it unearthly. And in truth I imagine that the sound resulted from no human will, but rather from those spasmodic forces which may act upon the form when life has ceased. . . . The shriek men heard rending the air was the shriek of a corpse."

On into the pen of fire rode the Light Brigade. Saddles emptied fast, and riderless horses, as is the manner of the poor brutes, ranged themselves on either side of the gallant leader, Lord Cardigan, and their hoofs thundered with the rest. Shrieks, curses, groans, and cheers were mingled as onward, ever onward, at racing speed, rode the brave band. Never once did Lord Cardigan turn in his saddle, but, erect and straight, flew over the grass, and, with eyes riveted on the crimson tunic of their leader, the gallant men followed him to death. Down went man and horse, with shriek, with prayer, and some without a sound, but never a pause in the devoted ranks.

"Now, my brave lads, for old England!" roared Sir George Paget, as they dashed towards the guns; onward, ever onward, till at length the guns were reached, and those who were left rode in behind them cutting and thrusting at the gunners with a maniacal fury.

Lord Cardigan has described the dull wonder with which he found himself unhit by the discharge of a twelve-pounder almost in his face, and the next instant cutting and slashing at the men who fired it. Eyewitnesses have described the awful sights seen after the charge; of the charge itself few can speak with accuracy.

Says a private soldier of the Black Watch, who by this time had arrived upon the scene:—

> A Russian gunner was holding his head together. It had been struck with a cavalry sword. He was alive, and was walking to the front, when my comrade called out, 'Don't take him to the front, take him to the rear; our doctors may make something of him.' He was sent to the rear holding his head together. It was often spoken of years afterwards in our regiment.

The same man, Alexander Robb of Dundee, says:—

> I saw one of the Greys, holding his arm that was nearly cut through. He also was able to walk. As he was passing us, he said, 'They say the Russians are not good at the sword, but I never gave a point but I got a parry,' and he made his way, laughing, to the surgeons.

Thus were the guns taken at Balaclava. "It was magnificent, but it was not war," said General Bosquet. The position was untenable, and after a few brief instants the order came "Threes about, retire!" and back rode the shattered force—195 mounted men in all. Once more the Russian fire broke out, and that the carnage on the return journey down the north valley was not heavier was due entirely to the French cavalry, the gallant *Chasseurs d'Afrique*. Realising the urgent danger of the Light Brigade, they diverted the attention of the right-hand Russian battery upon themselves, and thus doubtless preserved many lives in the ranks of the sadly thinned six hundred.

That the whole charge of the Light Brigade was a grievous error none could deny, least of all Lord Raglan, who angrily demanded of Lord Cardigan, as the scattered remnant of the cavalry reformed— "What did you mean, sir, by attacking a battery in front, contrary to all the usages of war?" It is, however, not unpleasing to learn that, writing privately of the charge, Lord Raglan has described it as "perhaps the finest thing ever attempted!"

With the charge of the Light Brigade, which lasted some twenty minutes, the battle practically ended, and about four o'clock the firing ceased. The Russians still held the captured redoubts, and had indeed succeeded in severing Balaclava, from the main allied camps before Sebastopol, but no strategical advantage could dim the lustre and the glorious prestige of the hare-brained charge of Lord Cardigan and the Light Cavalry.

Lord Lucan was removed from the command of the cavalry of the

"Army of the East," and his request to be tried by court-martial was refused.

The allied and Russian losses at Balaclava were nearly equal in number—between 600 and 700 on either side.

CHAPTER 13

The Battle of Inkerman: 1854

By the first week of November enormous numbers of reinforcements reached the Russian Army in the Crimea, so that not only were some 120,000 troops under Prince Mentschikoff's command, but a corresponding enthusiasm was awakened amongst all Russian ranks by this large addition to their numbers. Such warlike enthusiasm received a great impetus at this time by the arrival in camp of two young grand dukes, Michael and Nicholas, sons of the *Czar*.

The allied troops, on the other hand, had by this time an effective strength of some 65,000 men, and with an extended line of nearly 20 miles to guard it was apparent to all that a severe struggle for supremacy would shortly take place.

As is so often the case in war, those upon the spot, Lord Raglan and General Camobert, though fully aware of a large accession to the enemy's strength, were not so well posted as to its precise extent as were their fellow-countrymen in France and England. In both countries intense anxiety prevailed as to the outcome of the next engagement of the war.

They were not long kept in suspense. The Russian plan of attack comprised a general advance, partly a feint, upon the allied right, simultaneous with a sortie from the city of Sebastopol. Sunday, the 5th November, was the day fixed upon.

On the eve of the battle—the night of the 4th November—and again as early as four o'clock on the morning of the 5th, the bells of Sebastopol were heard ringing, and it was afterwards ascertained that the Russian Church was bestowing her blessing upon the soldiers of the *Czar*. Moreover, the clangour of the great bells to some extent covered the sound of the footsteps of the advancing hordes as they crept forward to the attack some hours before sunrise.

The attack was admirably planned. The extreme southernmost

portion of the Russian Army, under Prince Gortschakoff, was to feint an attack against the Guards and the French under Bosquet, thereby hindering them from marching to the assistance of our 2nd Division under General Pennefather, in whose charge lay the district of Mount Inkerman. Mount Inkerman itself, the real objective of the enemy, was to be assailed by 40,000 men under General Dannenburg. To the north again, the Sebastopol garrison was to effect a further diversion, engaging the allied left.

Upon the 2nd Division then was to fall the brunt of the fight, for the possession of the high ground of Mount Inkerman would enable the Russians to overlook their besieging enemy, hamper their operations, and, in all probability, compel them to abandon the siege.

On the afternoon of the 4th, General Pennefather, who commanded the 2nd Division, in the absence through illness of Sir de Lacy Evans, going his rounds as usual, observed a somewhat increased activity on the part of the enemy, but not of such a nature as to warrant other than ordinary vigilance. Towards evening a thick mist and heavy drizzle set in, and the outlying pickets on Mount Inkerman strained their eyes through the mist and darkness for a possible glimpse of the enemy. Captain Sargent, indeed, of the 95th, regarded the night as being specially favoured to an attack by the enemy, and increased the vigilance of the picket under his command, reloading some of the wetted rifles with his own hands. Towards four o'clock there rang out the pealing of the Sebastopol bells aforementioned, and several men reported that they distinctly heard the rumbling of waggon or gun-carriage wheels during the early hours of the morning.

With all these premonitions, however, the attack came suddenly, so favoured were the enemy by mist and darkness.

Shortly after the changing of the pickets, and just as day was breaking, a sentry of the outermost picket on Mount Inkerman stood straining his eyes to pierce the mist that lay around him dim and silent. Suddenly it seemed to him a part of it towards the Shell Hill became darker than the rest, and then slowly began to move towards him. The sentry rubbed his eyes, thinking he must be dreaming, but sure enough the dark patch moved slowly up towards him out of the ravine, making never a sound, so thick and deadening lay the mist.

Instantly he dashed off to his officer in command, Captain Rowlands, and reported his suspicions, and together in the now rapidly-clearing mist they beheld the approach of not one, but two Russian battalions in array of battle. *Bang!* rang out the picket's fire, and firing

BATTLE OF INKERMAN

obstinately, disputing every inch of the ground, it fell back before the now rapidly-advancing foe. The Inkerman engagement had begun.

Quickly the sound of firing roused the camp, and a battery was at once established on a shoulder known as Home Ridge, to check the enemy's advance by firing more or less at random into the mist. Shortly afterwards, Lord Raglan and General Camobert appeared on the scene and placed an increased battery at General Pennefather's disposal.

By intermittent firing, stubborn resistance, and occasionally a bayonet charge, the advancing Russian columns were thrown back behind their guns, which were by this time posted on Shell Hill.

The respite was not for long. A force of more than 10,000 Russians under General Sornionoff in person next swarmed up in front of Pennefather's devoted troops now slightly augmented by General Adams and the 41st regiment. Again, and again did overwhelming masses of Russians pit themselves, with hoarse cries, against numerically insignificant bodies of our troops. Reports have it that the Russian soldiers had been sent into battle inflamed by large quantities of raw spirit, and certainly the extraordinary violence and pertinacity of their attack tends to support this belief.

Be this as it may, their most determined onslaughts proved unavailing. With sword, bayonet, and, where the brushwood was too thick to admit of hand-to-hand fighting, with rifle ball, did our brave fellows drive them back, and many a Victoria Cross was won in the detached, but none the less effective fighting of this the first stage of the long Inkerman fight.

Here was Townsend's battery lost and recaptured. Here Lieutenant Hugh Clifford won his cross "for valour," leading some seventy men right into the heart of a column which threatened to turn his flank. Here Nicholson and many another gallant officer was killed; whilst, in this part of the field, Colonel Egerton, with some 260 men, totally routed and relentlessly pursued 1,500 of the famous Tomsk regiment.

Kinglake tells the story briefly:—

'There are the Russians, General,' said Egerton to General Buller, as the great grey mass loomed before them in the mist; 'what shall we do?' 'Charge them!' retorted Buller tersely. And charge them he did with a will, hurling them down the hillside with loud hurrahs, and following their confused and broken ranks with sword and bayonet.

Thus, again were the Russians beaten back from the slopes of Ink-erman, and in the melee General Sornionoff himself was killed.

The next attack came from another quarter, but still the brunt of the fighting fell on Pennefather's troops.

Meanwhile, in other parts of the field, the Russians had carried out their admirable and well-laid plan of attack. Gortschakoff's forces had threatened Bosquet and the Guards who were opposing him. The Duke of Cambridge, however, who commanded in that part of the field, was not long deceived by the feints of the enemy. Leaving only the Coldstreams to face Gortschakoff (and withdrawing even these before long), he hurried the grenadiers and Scots Fusiliers to Pennefather's assistance. Bosquet also perceived Inkerman to be the real point of attack, and while still facing Gortschakoff with his troops, held them in readiness to march thither should the need arise, as it very soon did.

Sir Colin Campbell's forces, however, were detained near Balaclava in a state of inaction, to protect that important port; as it happened an unnecessary, but very wise, provision.

Says one of the garrison under Sir Colin:—

We remained in the trenches under arms for three or four hours. The whole Balaclava force was under arms in the same manner, while Sir Colin was riding along the line of trenches and keeping an eye on the enemy in front, which (*sic*) appeared to be threatening an attack on us. We heard a heavy musketry fire from the front, and it was well on in the day before it slackened, and the enemy were seen to move backwards, out of sight—all but their sentries. We remained the same, however, not knowing what was up.

On the Sevastopol front, on the other hand, nothing of importance happened till, between nine and ten o'clock, a resolute sortie under General Timovieff took place, and th attention of Prince Napoleon was so occupied with this attack, which at one time met with some measure of success, that his troops were unable to reach Mount Inkerman in time to take part in the main fight.

Thus, it will be seen that in this part of the field the enemy attained his object and made a successful division. All other troops available were despatched with speed to the scene of the main action on Inkerman.

Of Mount Inkerman itself it may be said that it is in the shape of a long narrow triangle, with base towards the Russians and joined towards the Chersonese by its apex to the high ground of the British camps—this narrow neck being known as the Isthmus. Shell Hill forms its highest point, whilst on either hand, but nearer the allied camp, are lesser heights or shoulders called respectively Home Ridge and English Heights, and lying north and south of the central peak of Shell Hill, and separated from it by a ravine. A lower ridge between these two was called the Fore Ridge, upon which at either end were the slight defences of the Barrier and Sandbag Battery, both destined ere long to become famous—"the scene of one of the bloodiest combats in history."

For now, once more the Russians swarmed up in front of our already hard-pressed outposts, the clearer atmosphere revealing their true and overwhelming numbers.

By this time the grenadiers and Scots Fusiliers, under the Duke of Cambridge, were rapidly approaching. And now began that terrific struggle over the Sandbag Battery which resulted in that comparatively worthless entrenchment, situated as it was some yards in advance of the British position, being taken and retaken many times with awful slaughter on both sides.

Pennefather's brave fellows, General Adams and his brigade, the Guards, and some of the French infantry waged in turn a fierce war round the comparatively worthless position, and soon its shallow trench was heaped with dead and dying. Time and again the Russians would sweep into the battery, with murder in their eyes and brain, and bayonet any hapless wounded left behind perforce by our outnumbered men. A few brief moments would elapse, our gallant fellows would re-form, and, tooth and nail, with cold steel and even fist to face they would drive out the invader and hunt the Russians down the slope, thence only to return with dogged pertinacity again and again to the assault.

The 56th Westmoreland, the 41st Welsh, the 49th Herefordshire, the 20th and 95th, the grenadiers, Scots Fusiliers and grenadiers again—each in turn occupied for varying intervals of time the worthless battery, and then were either forced by weight of numbers to retire or else abandoned the battery themselves, having discovered its incapacity for shelter. Seven times in all was the battery captured by the Russians, and seven times retaken by our men.

Says the great historian of the war:—

123

The parapet of the Sandbag Battery—it stands to this day—(1869) is a monument of heroic devotion and soldierly prowess, yet showing, as preachers might say, the vanity of human desires. Supposed, although wrongly, to be a part of the British defences, and fought for, accordingly, with infinite passion and at a great cost of life by numbers and numbers of valiant infantry, the work was no sooner taken than its worthlessness became evident, not indeed to the bulk of the soldiery, but to those particular troops which chanced to be posted within it.

And so, the mistaken fight raged on, and heavy indeed were the losses around the fateful battery. The dead lay around in heaps.

Here General Adams died, his ankle shattered by a Russian bullet, and General Torrens was here so grievously wounded that he died later. As he lay upon the ground, General Sir George Cathcart rode down to him, crying, "Well and gallantly done, Torrens!" only to fall himself within the hour, a bullet through his heart.

Many are the gallant deeds and hairbreadth escapes recounted from this quarter of the field. The Duke of Cambridge only escaped being cut off by the Russians through dint of hard riding, a horse being killed under him and a bullet grazing his arm. Here Burnaby and his brave little party were some moments surrounded on every side, and only rescued by the French 7th battalion of the line; and here and there "General Pennefather's favourite oaths could be heard roaring cheerily down through the smoke" as he galloped from point to point, encouraging his men wherever the stress was greatest. It was at this time a horse was killed under him, throwing him to the ground in its fall, and men smiled amid the slaughter as they heard the old general "damning" the Russian gunners with all the fervour of his years!

On both sides reinforcements were hurried up continually, and regiment after regiment distinguished itself. "Men! remember Albuera!" rang out the voice of young Captain Stanley of the (57th, as a bullet! tore its way into his heart, and his devoted company sprang forward over his body, upholding to the last the splendid tradition of the "Die Hards."

At length, about 8.30, the vast hordes of General Dannenburg were pressed back, and something of a lull occurred. The British still held their ground, but with a frightful loss of nearly 1,500 men.

From this time forward the Russian attack was mainly directed at the Home Ridge, and for a while it prospered. In this part of the field the allied forces consisted of some 2,000 British, with a regiment of French and a small body of *Zouaves*, who had joined the Inkerman fight without orders, and for pure love of fighting. Most opportune was the moment of the arrival of this little body of troops, for without hesitation they hurled themselves at a Russian force which in the first brief moments of the onslaught had captured three British guns in advance of the position, and triumphantly restored them to their owners. Kinglake has declared his belief that they were led by Sir George Brown in person, who had discovered them wandering leaderless in a remote portion of the field.

Meanwhile the main body of the Russians advanced, covered by the heavy fire of their artillery on Shell Hill. So heavy indeed was this fire that Lord Raglan and the headquarters staff were in serious clanger by reason of it. As Lord Raglan was directing the movements of the troops from the rear of the British lines, a round shot tore the leg off General Strangeways, with whom he was conversing. Without a cry the old man begged to be assisted from his horse, for he did not lose his grip of the saddle, and was led tenderly to the back of the fight, where he died a veteran soldier of Wellington's. At the same instant a shell burst, blowing the horses of two more staff officers to pieces, and splashing the headquarters staff with blood.

Lord Raglan had been too often under fire to be in any way perturbed by these events, and never for an instant did he relax his grip upon the battle. It was well indeed that he did not, for the Russians were making headway, and at this critical juncture, the 7th Léger, a young French battalion, showed signs of weakening. The French officers, however, never lacking in bravery, beat their men back into line, and, mingled with the remnant of the 56th, literally shoulder to shoulder, the French and British faced, and ere long worsted, the foe.

Back and forwards raged the fight at the Barrier. Now the Russians were in retreat; now for want of fresh troops to press the victory home the pursuit weakened, and they rallied and returned; now they were driving our men back, and all the while their artillery from Shell Hill poured down a pitiless rain of lead upon our wearied troops, and sometimes even on their own front ranks, so close and intermingled was the fighting at this point.

Lord Raglan, ever upon the alert, beheld the weakening of our tired-out forces, and sent a staff officer post haste to Bosquet, bidding him at once bring up supports in force. Meanwhile, as at the Alma, here Raglan changed the whole aspect of the fight by the sudden bringing into action of two guns.

"Bring up two 18-pounders!" came the order, and with crack of whip and mingled oaths and cheers, two of these, our most powerful pieces of ordnance, under the command of Colonel Collingwood Dickson, were placed in position on the ridge, and soon the thunderous fire of nearly a hundred of the enemy's cannon became intermittently punctuated with the deep roar of the 18-pounders. Shot after shot from these missive guns tore whistling across the intervening valley and ploughed their deadly way through flesh and blood, here wiping out a group of Russian gunners, here dismounting a gun, there blowing up an. ammunition waggon, till in a brief half-hour the formidable artillery on Shell Hill began to slacken fire.

Many a British gunner was killed in this artillery duel, for the Russian fire was of course drawn against their new assailants, but eager volunteers pressed forward, and the guns were well and nobly served. So good in fact was their practice, and so great the havoc they wrought amongst the Russians, that Colonel Dickson's battery was specially mentioned in the official records of the battle "for its distinguished and splendid service."

After the distress put upon the Russians by the "18-pounder" battery—one shot of which narrowly missed Prince Mentschikoff and the two young grand dukes, who were watching the fight from the rear of the Russian position the end was not long in coming. Led by their *"vivandiére*, gaily moving in her pretty costume, fit alike for dance or battle," the *Zouaves* made a dash forward, and hurled themselves upon the enemy with the bayonet. At this moment a number of the Coldstreams joined the *Zouaves*, and together rushed into the fray. The luckless Russians turned to flee, but soon found themselves hemmed in by the dead-strewn parapet of the Sandbag Battery. The victorious French and British drove them back as sheep are driven to a pen, and slaughtered all they could lay hands on. The *Zouave* standard was planted above the embrasure, heaped about with bodies.

From now onwards the war was carried into the enemy's lines. Finding the Russian artillery fire dwindling, our troops at the Barrier pressed forward. Step by step, in little knots and companies, our men pressed up the hill, and many a gallant deed was done in this the final stage.

Lieutenant Acton of the 77th rushed forward for some few moments with only one private soldier of his company, to the capture of a Russian battery. An instant later, the whole body followed their brave and impetuous leader, and pressing up the hill reached the battery only in time to see the last gun limbered up.

Here a knot of British would fling themselves upon a company of Russians with the bayonet, and heavy slaughter on both, sides would result, but ever upward and forward pressed the victorious advance, the men faint with hunger but vigorous in pursuit, while the French engaged the Russian forces in the flank. Suddenly it was observed that the Russian batteries were being withdrawn in haste, and General Codrington, watching the fight from the far side of Careenage Ravine, glanced at his watch and found the time to be a quarter to one.

By one o'clock, in fact, the battle was practically over, for there was no pursuit worth mentioning, General Camobert, himself wounded in the arm, declining to throw French troops too far forward unsupported—an omission which he afterwards deeply regretted. Prince Mentschikoff was furious when he beheld the soldiers of the *Czar* in full retreat, and angrily asked General Dannenburg by whose orders the retreat was taking place. The general's answer was short and sharp—retreat was necessary to avert disaster! Long and bravely had the Russian soldiers fought, but more than that they could not do.

By three o'clock Mount Inkerman was freed from Russian troops, and Lord Raglan and General Camobert rode side by side over the bloodstained field, strewn with the dead and dying of three nations; and Kinglake tells how the British commander-in-chief himself held up, with his one hand, the head of a wounded Russian soldier, parched with thirst, and begged water from his staff for the unhappy foeman. But there was no water on Mount Inkerman, and the poor wretch had to endure for many hours ere succour came.

Nearly 11,000 Russians lay dead upon the slopes of Inkerman 256 officers being amongst the killed; 2,357 British were put out of action 597 being killed, 39 of the number being officers. Indeed, the ten British generals on the field were either killed, wounded, or had their horses shot under them in action Lord Raglan alone escaping unscathed. Days were spent in burying the dead.

CHAPTER 14

The Siege of Sebastopol: 1854-55

Experts have declared that had Sebastopol been assaulted within two days of the Battle of the Alma, it would have fallen an easy prey to the Allied Armies of France and Britain. History has shown, however, that this was not done, and that instead, Sebastopol was attacked from the south—the side remote from the Alma; and even at this point not until many days had elapsed.

The time thus granted to Russia was not wasted by those of her subjects who garrisoned the beleaguered town. Under that prince of engineers, Colonel de Todleben, defence works were constructed with an almost superhuman activity, whilst the harbour mouth was blocked to the allied fleet by the simple expedient of sinking Russian ships of war across the bar. This desperate measure was long opposed by many in the councils of Sebastopol, but once decided upon it was promptly carried out. It has been reported that many Russian sailors wept as they watched their finest ships of war settling down in the green waters of the Sebastopol roadstead, and it may be well believed that this was so, for the love of the sailor for his ship is proverbial. The Russian sailors showed no ignoble grief.

The roadstead of Sebastopol may be likened to a letter T, the top part of which constituted the roadstead proper, and the vertical portion the "man-of-war harbour." The Sevemaya, or north part of the town, was built along the top of the roadstead, and consisted almost entirely of fortifications. To the west of the man-of-war harbour lay the town proper, while to the east of it was the Karabel Fanbourg, or suburb. At the extreme eastern end of the roadstead flows in the Tchemaya River.

This, then, was the town to be defended by Russia against an assault from the south. Accordingly, a semi-circle of forts was erected from a point half-way between the man-of-war harbour and the mouth of the Tchemaya; touching at its centre the southernmost point of the harbour mentioned; and having its other extremity on the sea coast at the entrance to the main roadstead, where the sunken ships defended the waterway against the approach of the allied fleets. The main forts on this semi-circle were eight in number, from east to west in order comprising the Little Redan, the Malakoff, the Redan, Flagstaff Bastion, the Central Bastion, the Land Quarantine Bastion, the Sea. Quarantine Fort, and Artillery Fort—the last named being within the semi-circle of defence, to the east of the Sea Quarantine Fort.

These works of defence the Russians now toiled at day and night unceasingly.

Meanwhile the allies, having decided upon an extensive siege, in preference to an instant assault, actively pressed forward their siege works. Great difficulty was encountered by the engineers in their task of bringing their stores and battering trains some six or seven miles from the coast to their required position, the means of transport being poor. The heavy Lancaster guns had to be dragged overland by many sailors "tallyed on" to drag ropes, and progress was slow. Work in the trenches was heavy.

Eventually, on the morning of the 17th October, the first bombardment of Sebastopol commenced, the heavy Lancaster battery opening fire about 6 a.m. The noise was terrific, for very soon both allies and Russians were engaged in a tremendous artillery duel. The earth shook, dense volumes of smoke hung over Sebastopol and about the allies' batteries, and shot and shell flew screeching through the air. About midday, when the fleets joined in, the din was redoubled.

On both sides, losses, both in men and armament, were severe. Some would serve the guns; others, with pick and spade, would, under heavy fire, repair breaches in the earthworks; others would rush hither and thither with pails of water to extinguish fires which now and again broke out in the timber of the batteries; others again bore off the wounded on litters to a place of safety—but each and all worked with a will, and never for an instant did the terrific fire slacken.

Now and again the smoke would lift for a moment, and some measure of the damage done on either side would be hastily gauged. Great bravery was displayed by besiegers and besieged, and humour as usual found its way into such an incongruous place.

"I say, lads," said a young Scot, one of the redoubtable Black Watch; "I dinna think there'll be many kail-pots boiling in Sebastopol the day!" Nor were there!

The Russian admiral, Kornlinoff, over and over again exposed himself to shot and shell as he rode round from point to point of the defences, and at length so often was he bespattered with sand and stones thrown up on all sides from the earthworks, that he handed his watch over to a courier, telling him to give it to his wife. "I am afraid that here it will get broken," he added, humorously.

Before eleven o'clock the brave man had breathed his last. As he was descending the Malakoff after taking fresh instructions to the gunners of that fort, a shell tore his left thigh, and sadly *his aide-de-camp* and others bore him to the hospital. There, stretched upon a mattress of agony, the somewhat inaccurate news was brought him that the British guns were at length silenced, and with his last breath he cried "Hurrah!" dying, as he had lived, a brave man and noble foe.

Meantime in the French part of the field of action disasters had fallen thick and heavy. A well-directed Russian shell about nine o'clock burst in a French magazine on Mount Rodolph, the French main battery of attack, and with a terrific noise, heard even above the thunder of the arms, the men surrounding it were lifted sky high, the bodies falling round in dozens. A second explosion in the French lines just afterwards, silenced their land artillery for the day, the attack being maintained by the British artillery and by the allied fleets.

About half-past, one the French fleet opened fire from no less than six hundred guns—the Quarantine Sea Fort being the chief object of attack. Soon the other forts towards the sea were engaged by both navies, and awful havoc resulted on both sides.

All through the long October afternoon the battle raged, the cannonade from the sea being in the estimation of Admiral Dundas, the British commander, "the heaviest that had ever taken place on the ocean." Here again both sides suffered heavily, but the forts in the main suffered less than the vessels, many of which were greatly disabled, the *Albion* and *Arethusa* being completely crippled. The *Rodney* ran aground under the eye and well within the reach of Fort Constantine, and from her position right under the Russian gains maintained an obstinate fight till between six and seven, when the fleet hauled off and the naval bombardment was abandoned in the rapidly-fading light.

Little execution had been done by the fleets, but the disaster sustained by them was heavy, the British and French losing no fewer than 500 men killed and wounded, and moreover, failing in their attack.

Meantime, though the French batteries were out of action, the British land forces were making progress, and soon it became impossible for the Russians to repair the breaches in the embrasures of the Redan, though officers and men bent their backs alike to the work. Then, too, by reason of the heavy fire, the infantry supporting this important work fell back, and for a while the Redan was left defenceless, but the advantage was not pushed home before night fell and firing ceased. The turn of the Redan came later.

More than 1,000 Russians had been killed in this first day's bombardment, with but trifling advantage to the allies, so for the next few days the French proceeded to strengthen their attack, while the British batteries kept down to some extent the Russian fire. Thus, matters stood till the morning of the 25th October, when the allied rear attacked at Balaclava, and again, some ten days later, at Inkerman, on the 5th November. In both these contests the Russian lost heavily, but still the assault of Sebastopol was postponed, and it soon appeared that a Russian winter would have to be faced.

Life in the besieging trenches now became monotonous. Duties, as before, consisted of employment in working and covering parties, sharpshooting and picket work, and the long and dreary days were spent when off duty in one form of diversion and another, and many amusing incidents have been recounted, and many tales of suffering nobly borne been told.

A glimpse of the life of a private soldier at this time is very graphically recounted by one of the 42nd. Says this man in his published record:—

> The dismal time now commenced, for with digging and picking in the day time, and strong pickets at night, on poor rations, our clothing worn out and verminous, and the nearly worn-out bell tents to sleep in, on the cold bare ground, we were getting less in number every day. As the trenches were formed, we had to lie in them at night for the purpose of reinforcing the picket till the remainder turned out. We always had our rifles loaded, even the men in the tents, and false alarms were frequent. Even the poor rations were not half eaten. The pork and salt beef could be seen piled up at the tents untouched. . . But the commander-in-chief allowed us two rations of rum a day, and one extra on night duty.

The same man later says:—

> In the tent to which I belonged, to keep us from lying on the cold, wet mud, we got stones and lay upon them; they were

better to lie on than the wet ground!

Day by day the sound of the big guns reverberated through the camp, and day by day the victims of fever, dysentery, and shot and shell were borne to the hospitals at Kadikoi and Balaclava by the bandsmen and pipers, who were told off to this melancholy duty. An occasional reconnoitre in the intense frost of the Russian winter laid many a poor fellow low with frostbite, and with these and the aforementioned causes the hospitals soon grew full. The medical staff worked nobly, but were wholly inadequate, both in numbers and equipment, to cope with the enormous multitude of sick and wounded.

The worst cases were sent by ship to Scutari, where overcrowding also prevailed, in spite of the utmost efforts and the noble devotion of Miss Nightingale, at this time not long arrived from England.

A private soldier says:—

As I was going along the passages (of the Scutari hospital), which were full of patients, the rooms also being full, I was beginning to think no one cared for me, when a pleasant-looking lady approached and asked what was the matter with me, calling an orderly to get me into a bed. I was frequently visited by the lady, who was no less a person than Miss Nightingale.

So, in the camp and in the hospital the winter wore away with but two outstanding incidents; the great hurricane of the 14th November, and the engagement on the night of the 20th November at the "Ovens."

The hurricane of the 14th November did incalculable harm to all combatants. An hour before sunrise on that day the air was calm, and the wind had fallen after heavy rain the previous night. Suddenly a violent hurricane arose, accompanied by thunder, lightning, and sleet, and instantly all was pandemonium. Large trees were torn from their roots, practically every tent in the Allied Armies was blown flat, while roofs were carried away from houses in Sebastopol. Vast stores of forage were destroyed, and accounts state that at least one man was swept off his feet and carried some twenty yards by the sheer force of the wind! All day the elements held sway until evening, when the storm abated as quickly as it had arisen, and an intense calm prevailed, the stars shining out upon the miry, stricken camp.

Among the horses and the shipping, the casualties were heavy, and the loss sustained by the cyclone of the 14th was not repaired for many a long day.

The story of the capture of the "Ovens" is inseparably connected with the name of Lieutenant Tryon of the Rifle Brigade, who lost his life in the engagement. The "Ovens" comprised a series of old Tartar caves and stone huts long since untenanted, but now used with deadly effect by Russian riflemen as "cover," whence they could annoy the French working parties. Becoming in course of time unbearable by reason of the accuracy of their fire, it was determined to dislodge them, the task being entrusted to Lieutenant Tryon and some men of the Rifle Brigade.

Feinting an open attack with half his men, Tryon, on the night of the 20th November, crept with the other half, stealthily upon the Russians, surprised them into a retreat, and established himself in the very caves which the Russians had vacated. Their retreat was not for long, and very soon they returned in overwhelming numbers to the attack, and three times were they repelled by Tryon and his gallant band. Eventually "supports" arrived to the Rifles, and the "Ovens" were held by our men, to the great admiration of the French. Tryon, however, was mortally wounded by a Russian bullet.

After the affair at the "Ovens" the dull routine went on as before, and sickness did its deadly work amongst the armies of the three combatant nations.

The British Government seemed wholly unable to cope with the requirements of its army in the Crimea, and the tale of the winter's misery has been told by many. The improper food, wretched shelter, inadequate clothing, and deficient medical supplies have been emphasised by hundreds, and small wonder that privation and disease wrought as terrible havoc as did the shot and shell of the enemy.

Towards the end of December, an improvement began to be effected. The women of Britain, from the sovereign downwards, toiled unceasingly to remedy the defective clothing and increase the comfort of the soldiers, and moreover, wooden huts were erected in place of the now worn-out tents, so that by the arrival of spring the troops were in a better position to carry on their arduous work. Moreover, fresh troops were constantly arriving, and Sardinia furnished a powerful contingent to her new made allies of France and Britain.

Still, with all these advantages, the awful monotony of the siege weighed upon the stoutest of our men, and any diversion was eagerly welcomed.

On the 2nd March, 1855, the Emperor Nicholas died, worn out, it has been said, in body and soul by the protracted struggle in the south of his dominions, and, in particular, by the reverses sustained by his troops in Eupatoria at the hands of the Turks. But the death of the *Czar* had little effect upon the war in the Crimea. His successor, Alexander, prosecuted the defence with unabated energy. In May an expedition to Kertch harassed the Russians considerably, while the newly-arrived Sardinians, in conjunction with the French, obtained a signal success on the Tchemaya.

These were, however, but side issues, and the main armies maintained their dreary watch upon Sevastopol, where work and counter-work, mine and countermine, employed the ingenuities of the engineers of both nations.

The appearance of Sebastopol at this time has been ably shown by Mr. Conolly in his history of the Royal Engineers:—

> Parallels and approaches now covered the hills, and saps daringly progressed in front; dingy pits filled with groups of prying and fatal marksmen, studded the advances and flanks; caves were augmented in size and number in the sides of the ravines to give safety to the gunpowder, . . . while new works were thrown up in front to grapple with the sturdy formations of the Russians.

Sorties by the enemy were frequent, and, on the night of the 22nd March, a most determined attack was made upon the working parties of the allies from four different points. It failed, however, to accomplish much, and matters continued as before.

On Monday, the 9th April, another terrific bombardment occurred, the British gunners directing their special attention to the Flagstaff Bastion. For several days, until the 18th April, the battery was plied mercilessly with shot and shell, and reduced to a state of distress bordering on annihilation; it still, however, remained unassaulted, and during a temporary truce was patched up once more. On the 21st, however, its fire was reduced to complete silence.

Count Tolstoy in his stirring pictures of "Sevastopol," so admirably translated by Louise and Aylmer Maude, has given us a vivid glimpse of affairs in this awful battery, "the Fourth Bastion," as the Russians called it. Tolstoy, showing an imaginary visitor through the beleaguered town says:—

> You want to get quickly to the Bastions, especially to that Fourth Bastion of which you have been told so many tales. When anyone says, 'I am going to the Fourth Bastion,' a slight

agitation or a too marked indifference is always noticeable in him! When you meet someone carried on a stretcher, and ask, 'Where from?' the answer usually is, 'From the Fourth Bastion.' Passing a barricade, you go up a broad street. Beyond this the houses on both sides of the street are unoccupied, the doors are boarded up, the windows smashed, . . . on the road you stumble over cannonballs that lie about, and into holes full of water, made in the stony ground by bombs. Before you, up a steep hill, you see a black, untidy space cut up by ditches. This space is the Fourth Bastion. The whiz of cannonball or bomb nearby impresses you unpleasantly as you ascend the hill, bullets begin to whiz past you right and left, and you will perhaps consider whether you had better not walk inside the trench which runs parallel to the road, full of yellow stinking mud more than knee-deep!

To reach the bastion proper:—

You turn to the right, along that narrow trench where a foot soldier, stooping down, has just passed, and where you will see Cossacks changing their boots, eating, smoking their pipes and, in fact, living! Soon you come to a flat space with many holes and cannons on platforms and walled in with earthworks. This is the bastion. Here you see perhaps four or five soldiers playing cards under shelter of the breastwork, and a naval officer sitting on a cannon rolling a cigarette composedly. Suddenly a sentinel shouts 'Mortar!' There is a whistle, a fall, and an explosion, mingled with the groans of a man. You approach him as the stretchers are brought; part of his breast has been torn away; in a trembling voice he says, 'Farewell, brothers.'
'That's the way with seven or eight every day,' says the officer, and he yawns as he lights another cigarette.

In the British trenches similar scenes were being enacted, the same coolness under fire, and resolute contempt of clanger being displayed by all ranks and nationalities.

A Highland soldier wrote to his parents:—

One day there was a cluster of us together, when a shell fell close by. The fuse was not exhausted when John Bruce up with it in his arms and threw it over the trench.

Such incidents were by no means rare, and in this wise the summer wore on with varying fortune. In May the command of the French Army was taken up by General Pélissier, and on the 28th June the master-mind of the British Army was removed—Lord Raglan, beloved and mourned by all ranks, dying of cholera after a brief two days' illness. Kinglake has recorded how on the morning on the 29th, the commander-in-chief of the four Allied Armies visited the chamber of death, and how the iron frame of the staunch General Pélissier shook with grief as he "stood by the bedside for upwards of an hour crying like a child."

On board the *Caradoc* the body of the field-marshal was conveyed to England, and all ranks mourned for one whom they had learnt to trust, admire, and almost love "so noble, so pure, so replete with service rendered to his country." For seven miles the route of the procession to the *Caradoc* was lined at either side by double ranks of infantry, and, says the historian of the war, during the melancholy march:—

> French, and British refrained from inviting by fire the fire of Sebastopol, and whether owing to chance, or to a signal and grateful act of courtesy on the part of General Ostin-Sacken (now in command), the garrison also kept silence.

So died Lord Raglan, and the command of the British troops now vested on General Sir James Simpson, a veteran of the Peninsular.

On the morning of the 5th September, the final bombardment of Sebastopol commenced, and the terrific cannonade continued till the 8th. The French were the first to open fire, and they did so with a will. Once more the deafening thunder of the heavy guns and shrieks of shell and mortar were heard about Sebastopol, and ere long the cannonade wrought fearful havoc with the "churches, stately mansions, and public buildings of the still imposing-looking city."

From nearly three miles of batteries poured forth the devastating fire, and a storm of iron swept across the doomed town. Buildings could be seen crashing down, large spouts of earth rose high into the air, and, with the glasses, stretcher-bearers could be seen busy at every point.

British and French alike were soon engaged, the Russian return fire being for a long time paralysed by the fury of the onslaught. The Redan and the Malakoff were the particular objectives of the British fire, and soon the faces of these mighty works were seen pitted "as if with the smallpox."

At night a musketry fire was kept up to hinder the Russians from repairing their shattered walls and bastions, till, by the 8th, all was ready for a final and vigorous assault.

The assault was to be in two portions; the French were to capture the Malakoff, and, on attaining this their object, were to signal by rocket fire the fact of its accomplishment. The British were then to assault the Redan, which was connected to the Malakoff by a series of trenches.

Noon was the hour fixed for the Malakoff assault. By half-past eleven the supports were all in readiness. The Guards were posted on the Woronzoff Road, part of the 4th Division was in the trenches, the 3rd Division was held in readiness, while the Highland Brigade, under Sir Colin Campbell, was marched in from Kamara.

Says one of them:—

> We had marched nine miles in line of march order, but when we came to our old camp ground we took off our knapsacks, and put ourselves in trench order, only we were in the kilt. . . . We went into the trenches assigned for us to form the support. As I looked towards the Malakoff the French were going in, column after column. . . . They appeared to be keen to be in action.

Dr. Russell tells the story more graphically:—

> At five minutes before twelve o'clock, the French, like a swarm of bees, issued from their trenches close to the doomed Malakoff, scrambled up its face, and were through the embrasures in the twinkling of an eye. They took the Russians by surprise, and their musketry was very feeble at first, but they soon recovered themselves, and from twelve o'clock till past seven in the evening the French had to meet and repulse the repeated attempts of the enemy to regain the work. . . . At length, despairing of success, the Muscovite general withdrew his exhausted legions.

The retreat was by way of the Redan, which our men now prepared to assault.

> As soon as the tricolour was observed waving through the smoke and dust, over the parapet of the Malakoff, four rockets were sent up as a signal for our assault upon the Redan. They were almost borne back by the violence of the wind, and the silvery jet of sparks they threw out on exploding were scarcely visible against the raw grey sky.

The force selected for the attack was composed as follows:—160 men of the 3rd Buffs under Captain F. F. Maude, with 160 of the 77th under Major Welshford. These constituted the scaling-ladder party. Covering them were 100 more of the Buffs led by Captain John Lewes, with 100 of the 2nd battalion of the Rifles led by Captain Hammond. The remainder of the force comprised 260 of the Buffs, 300 of the 41st, 200 of the 62nd, with a working party of a hundred more. The 47th and 49th regiments were in reserve, together with Warren's brigade.

To Colonel Unset of the 19th fell the honour of leading the gallant' party into the fray, and at the outset he fell, badly wounded.

Sharp came the order: "Forward! ladders to the front; eight men per ladder!" and instantly our devoted men crept from the shelter of their trenches to the assault. At a furious pace they dashed up the slope leading to the Redan, and planted several ladders in the ditch against the wall.

But the slaughter was terrific. In less than a minute the slope of the Redan was thickly covered with red coats. In the ditch itself matters were worse. Wounded and dead, bleeding and shapeless, screaming or silent, our men lay heaped in scores, and still the murderous fire poured down from every window and embrasure in the work.

To add to the terrors of their position, our men were now met by overwhelming numbers, who streamed down the trenches from the abandoned Malakoff to the assistance of their comrades in the Redan, the scaling ladders; were found to be too short, and after an hour and a half of a disastrous fight our men fell back upon their trenches, firing steadily, but, for the time being, worsted.

The slaughter had been awful. Colonel Handcock of the Perthshire regiment, Captains Hammond, Preston, Corry and Lockhart, Colonel James Ewan of the 41st, and others too numerous to mention lay dead upon the slope or within the fatal Redan, where many of our men had penetrated in the first fierce rush, and scarcely a man was unbounded.

After this set back, it was decided to attack again at five a.m.—this time with the Guards and Highlanders.

One of them says:—

As the night wore on, the Highland Brigade advanced and took up position in the advanced trench, and we kept up a sharp fire with our rifles. Sir Colin came along the trenches later, and came down to where we were (by this time) making a new trench. I heard him say: 'That is your job in the morning,' pointing to the Redan.

But the attack was not to be. While searching for wounded comrades, Corporal John Ross of the Sappers wandered far from our foremost lines, and suddenly becoming aware of the absence of the Russian outpost, he crept forward up the slope and entered the Redan! The place was empty! The Russians had deserted it earlier in the evening, and the retreat from Sevastopol was even then begun.

Graphically Tolstoy has described it:—

> Along the whole line of the bastions no one was to be seen. All was dead, ghastly, terrible, but not silent; the destruction still went on. Everywhere on the ground, blasted and strewn around by fresh explosions, lay shattered guncarriages, crushing the corpses of foes and Russians alike. Bombs and cannon-balls and more dead bodies, then holes and splintered beams, and again silent corpses in grey and blue and red uniforms. . . . The Sebastopol Army, surging and spreading like the sea on a rough night, moved through the dense darkness, slowly swaying by the bridge (of boats) over the roadstead away from the place which it had held for eleven months, but which it was now commanded to abandon without a struggle. . . . On reaching the north side, almost every man took off his cap and crossed himself.

In the grey dawn of a Sunday morning, the Allied Armies entered the abandoned city. The Russians blew up magazine after magazine as they left the city, and it was sheeted in flame as the allies entered into possession of it. The fleet was even then settling down in the lurid waters of the harbour, scuttled by the retreating foe.

In the Redan many a British soldier was found stark and stiff with outstretched hand upon a Russian's throat; some were even found clinging to the parapet as if alive! One of the most heroic episodes recalled with the assault of the Redan is that of Lieutenant Massy of the 19th, who, to hearten his men, stood long exposed in the open to the heaviest Russian fire. Though badly wounded he survived, being long known among his countrymen as "Redan Massy."

Though Sevastopol had fallen, it was not till the last day of February, 1856, that an armistice was concluded with Russia. Shortly before eight o'clock on that day a telegram reached the Russian Army, then camped upon the north side of the Sevastopol roadstead, whither it had retreated, and announced the temporary peace. On Wednesday, the

2nd April, a salute of 101 guns announced the conclusion of the war.

By the 11th April preparations for the return home were commenced, and went briskly forward, but alas! how many stayed behind. No fewer than 130 cemeteries in the Crimea mark the last resting place of British dead; in the French great Campo Santo are 28,000 sons of France!

CHAPTER 15

The Battles of Bushire, Kooshab, and Mohammerah: 1856-57

It is a platitude to say that the kingdom of Afghanistan is, on its Asiatic side, the bulwark of British India. Yet upon this important, if well-known, fact depended the Persian campaign of 1856. A brief recapitulation of history will show clearly the causes which led to the British invasion.

On the fall of the Mogul dynasty in India, the plains of Afghanistan were divided between Persia and Hindoostan, but as the power of their conquerors gradually declined the Afghans rose, under Ahmed Shah, a native officer, and after a successful invasion of Hindoostan, in 1773, founded the modern Afghan kingdom. After varying fortunes, however, the only portion of the once famous kingdom that remained under the sway of Ahmed Shah's descendants was the principality and town of Herat. At this time Mohammed Shah ruled over Persia, and on Prince Kanwan of Herat refusing to pay his accustomed tribute to Persia, the *Shah* prepared to make war upon him.

Such a quarrel, while looked upon with great favour by Russia, could only end in the weakening of the British outposts of India, and, accordingly, Britain did all in her power to hinder the Persian expedition to Herat, while Russia fomented the quarrel. Through British influence, Herat proposed to submit to an arbitration by our government, but, egged on by Russia, the *Shah* declined to favour any half measures, and accordingly, in December, 1837, Herat was besieged by the forces of the *Shah*.

Well knowing the importance of Herat, and fearing for the consequences should it fall into the hands of Persia, our representatives strongly urged the interference of the British Government at this juncture.

Two other causes now combined to make critical the situation in Persia. One was the seizing by Persian high officials of a British envoy, returning from Herat; the other the personal insult offered by an, intoxicated Indian *dervish* in the town of Bushire to Mr. Gerald of the British residency. The man in question, without provocation, openly insulted Mr. Gerald in the street, ultimately knocking off his cap. Mr. Gerald very promptly retorted by severely handling his assailant, with the result that the latter appealed to the Governor of Bushire for redress. The British Government, on the other hand, demanded compensation for the insult to one of its representatives.

The tendency of these incidents was to put a severe strain upon Anglo-Persian relations, and at this time the activity of Russia was so marked that Mr. McNeill urged upon the government the advisability of some show of force to restore our prestige in the affected districts.

At length, therefore, a force from India was despatched to the island of Karrack, in the Persian Gulf, and a corresponding consternation was perceptible throughout Persia, while, at the same time, the *Shah* was given clearly to understand that the continued siege of Herat would lead to an open rupture with Great Britain.

For a time then, the siege of Herat was raised, and some form of apology tendered to the British Minister, but once more Russia (always, however, unofficially) stirred up the embers of war, which threatened at this period to cool.

Petty annoyances and minor outrages upon British subjects were at this time of constant occurrence, and at length Sir Frederick Maitland, commander-in-chief of our naval forces in India, on the 25th March, 1839, landed some men from the Wellesley at Bushire. These men were fired upon by the Persians, but, as the result of prompt action on the part of our troops, a serious affray was averted. On the 29th, however, Captain Hennell, the British resident, was conveyed to Karrack with his staff, it being deemed unsafe for any British officials to remain in the country unprotected.

Eventually, as a result of pressure and the refusal of the British Government to receive the Persian envoy to the queen's coronation, and other similar uncompromising measures, peace was more or less fully restored in 1841. But history proverbially repeats itself.

Russian influences were at work, and by 1856 the Persian Army, upon pretext of settling local quarrels, was once more in front of Herat, and subsequently captured it. This, with other petty annoyances

The Battle of Kooshab

too numerous to mention, led, in November of that year, to a definite declaration of war against the *Shah*.

As early as July or August, 1856, instructions had been sent to the Governor-General of India to collect at Bombay an adequate force, with transport, to occupy, in the event of negotiations breaking down, the island of Karrack and the city and district of Bushire, the commercial capital of Persia.

Says Captain Hunt, in his capital narrative of the Persian, campaign which he himself went through with his regiment, the 78th Highlanders:—

> Bushire is itself a place of much importance, and covers considerable ground. It is defended by a wall, and has no ditch. As a fortress it is inconsiderable—position and trade giving it all its value; and yet as a commercial town, none in the world has perhaps been oftener attacked.

Bushire, then, was the first objective of the British expedition, which, starting from Bunda Abbas in India, arrived in the Persian Gulf on the 29th November, 1856. Once in the roadstead, the British war vessels with their transports made so great a display of force that the Persian governor of the town despatched a messenger to Commander Jones, the then British Resident, "begging to be apprised of the object of their visit." Commander Jones's reply, which was addressed from the admiral's flagship, conveyed to the unlucky governor the scarcely welcome intelligence of the proclamation of war, and intimated that diplomatic relations were at an end.

The next move on the part of the British force was the occupation of Karrack Island, to the north of the town, an operation which met with no opposition, and then on the morning of 7th December preparations were made to disembark the troops in Kallila Bay, some ten miles to the south of Bushire.

Now at length the enemy began to show fight, and appeared in some force in a grove of date palms, near the spot chosen for disembarkation, but they were speedily driven from their positions. As our officers and men sat down to breakfast on the morning of the 7th, previous to disembarking, they were startled by a furious cannonade from the ships' guns, and, on going on deck to find the cause, discovered the grove of date palms in question to be the object of a heavy fire, which soon dislodged the Persians. From that time on the landing was effected without a casualty, the total firing occupying only a few minutes. A day was spent in resting the men, getting stores and so on, and by the morning of the 9th, General Stalker, who was in command, ordered a general advance towards the town of Bushire, the fleet meanwhile proceeding to approach the city from the sea, and holding itself in readiness to join in the attack.

Early in the morning an advance party proceeded to reconnoitre, and soon returned with the intelligence that a band of the enemy, some 400 strong, had entrenched themselves in the old Dutch fort of Reshire, which lay between our army and the town of Bushire. The enemy had opened fire with matchlocks upon our men.

The fort consisted largely of old houses and garden walls, and afforded good enough cover, so a general assault was ordered, the fort being encircled by our men except towards the sea, where cavalry were posted to cut down any of the enemy attempting to escape.

The columns of the 64th and 20th regiments under General Stopford advanced to the attack, and the enemy's fire at once became heavy. The affair was over in a few moments, and the Persians ran out at the rear of the work and up the beach, anywhere away from our rifles and bayonets, taking no heed of, or probably not understanding, the summons to surrender, and many were shot down while endeavouring to escape. General Stopford himself was killed by a bullet from a matchlock while leading the assault.

Colonel Malet, in command of the slender cavalry force, met his death by treachery. Seeing one of his troopers about to cut down a Persian who, kneeling on the beach, implored mercy with outstretched arms, Colonel Malet bade the trooper spare the wretch, and passed on. No sooner was his back towards the two when the Persian he had spared seized his matchlock from a bush where he had concealed it, and shot the colonel in the back.

Inside the fort many Persians were found hiding, and some of these were killed, while others made good their escape. Here also were found a large store of dates, of which our troops partook heartily, till a rumour was set on foot that they were poisoned. For some time considerable panic ensued, but the report was, to everyone's relief, proved to be unfounded.

Our troops then bivouacked near the captured fort, while the fleet, with our wounded on board, moved slowly and cautiously down towards Bushire to commence a bombardment following morning. In the meantime, Commander Jones had proceeded, in a small steamer carrying a flag of truce, to approach the town from the sea, with a view to summoning the Persian governor to an honourable surrender, but on entering the narrow channel leading to the roadstead he had been fired upon by the town batteries.

Accordingly, the orders were given to reverse engines, and Bushire lost its final opportunity of effecting an amicable settlement. Early on the following morning the sound of heavy firing from the town apprised the British camp at Reshire that the fleet had commenced their share of the day's operations. By nine o'clock the land force was under arms, and marched to within a mile of the land force of Bushire, where they were halted to await the issue of the bombardment.

This was not long in coming. Terrified by the heavy ordnance from the British warships, and paralysed by a sight of the land force, now drawn up in line and giving an extended front, the Persian Governor held a hurried council on the rampart.

A writer in *Blackwood's Magazine* of that period has given amusing extracts from that momentous conclave:—

'They stretch from sea to sea,' said one councillor. 'Their guns are innumerable,' said another; while a third observed, 'They will kill us all if we resist!'

Small wonder that the sadly perplexed and harassed governor decided, most humanely, that discretion was the better part of valour, and "pulled down his flag, or rather ordered the flagstaff to be cut down, agreeably to the inconvenient fashion of his country, which gives the victors the trouble of putting it up again."

The cannonade had lasted four hours and a half, but the damage done was slight, owing to the long range of firing necessitated by the shallow waters which surround the town, and it is worthy of note that the British Residency, which had been specially marked out to be avoided by our gunners, was in point of fact the most damaged building in the town!

So soon as the firing ceased, with the lowering of the Persian flag, General Stalker marched the land force into Bushire, and received the formal surrender of the town. As our men approached, many of the terrified Persians succeeded in making good their escape, while others were drowned in so doing. The remainder laid down their arms before the British lines, and to the number of nearly 2,000 regular troops were seated on the ground in rows. Thus, under a guard, they passed the night, and it is somewhat ludicrous to learn that every time the sharp words of command rang out for changing guard during the night, the valiant soldiers of the *Shah* bawled loudly for mercy, under the impression that their last hour had come!

In point of fact, in the morning they were set free, General Stalker deciding that it was useless to retain them prisoners.

The British casualties at the taking of Bushire were nil, the whole operation being effected by the guns of the fleet, though considerable gallantry was displayed by both soldiers and sailors.

As the low-lying marshy district of Bushire itself is far from healthy, the camp of the British Army of occupation was pitched some mile and a half from the city walls, and here, entrenched, our men awaited both the arrival of reinforcements and a possible Persian attack from Shiraz, where large numbers of troops were known to be collecting.

On the 30th January, 1857, the welcome reinforcements, the 2nd Division of the British Army in Persia, arrived in camp from Bombay, and with them appeared General Sir James Outram, in supreme command of the forces.

The accession of numbers due to the arrival of the 2nd Division brought up the strength of our army in Persia to some 3,500 men, with 18 guns. The new arrivals consisted of the 14th King's Light Dragoons, one troop of horse artillery, a thousand Scinde Horse, the 78th Highlanders, and two regiments of native infantry. Captain Hunt of the 78th, whose admirable record of the campaign is indeed the standard work upon the subject, was one of the incoming men, and he describes the state of the camp at Bushire at this time, and the uncertainty which prevailed as to the objective of future operations:—

> Supplies of all descriptions were plentiful in camp, and the inhabitants both of the town and neighbourhood were evidently pleased at the British occupancy; indeed they could scarcely be otherwise; for, irrespective of the pecuniary advantages of the presence of a large force which paid heavily, and on the spot, for everything, the orderly look and appearance of soldiers who visited the town, without even sidearms as a protection, contrasted most advantageously with the previous garrison, which had notoriously lived upon what could be stolen or extracted from the citizens.

Sir James Outram was not a man to let the grass grow under his feet, and it was by this time ascertained that a considerable Persian force was assembled at Shiraz, a town situated above the passes, some 150 miles from Bushire. Moreover, the Persian Government was known to have collected supplies of flour and ammunition at the villages of Borasjoon and Chakota, in the low country—the former forty, the latter twenty miles from Bushire.

Accordingly, on the afternoon of the 3rd February, towards evening, the entire force, with the exception of a camp guard, moved out of Bushire towards Chakota.

Here in the end of December General Stalker had already blown up a magazine of the enemy's ammunition, but had not deemed it necessary to occupy the town, preferring to direct his operations from Bushire.

At Chakota, then, arrived our now largely increased force by nine o'clock on the morning of the 4th February, and a halt of some hours was indulged in, the troops loading arms and making preparations for an immediate" engagement. By four o'clock the march was resumed, and the enemy's videttes in the neighbourhood of Borasjoon were sighted by noon on the following day.

The enemy had been steadily falling back, and up to the present our men had encountered nothing more formidable than heavy rain and thunderstorms. Now, however, the army was halted, positions for attack assigned, and final orders given, when, "to the disgust of all, the entire army in our front was descried in full retreat, and going off at such a pace as to render it hopeless to overtake them." Some of our cavalry, however, managed to get into touch with their rearguard, and a few wounds were received by our troopers.

The majority of the enemy, however, were quickly out of sight, having taken to the hills, where it was impossible to follow them, the hills hereabouts being "formidable and of great height, and, except at two or three pathways, utterly impassable."

The 6th and 7th were spent by our men in the enemy's vacated camp, during which time stores were destroyed and some treasure was discovered, together with many horses and carriage cattle.

An amusing incident was reported at this time. On the night of the 6th, an alarm was raised that the enemy was at hand, and in point of fact a half-hearted attack was commenced but came to nothing. During the "turn-out," however, the picket of one regiment, observing a suspicious appearance in the darkness ahead of them, surrounded the spot with extreme caution, and gallantly captured—an old house-door which had been accidentally left propped up against a bush! There was much laughter in the morning over this "daring exploit." On the night of the 7th, the return march to Bushire was commenced.

Up to midnight all went well, but shortly after, a sharp rattle of musketry was heard in the direction of the rearguard, and a halt was at once called. In about half an hour, however, all was pandemonium. Little could be seen, the night being intensely dark, but the enemy were heard screaming like fiends on every side. Horsemen galloped almost up to our lines, bugles were blown, and everything done to cause confusion. From the first, moment of attack our troops behaved with admirable steadiness. The necessary movements were perfectly executed, in spite of the darkness, and the formation of a hollow square, in which to await the break of day, was rapidly performed.

Sir James Outram himself was, in the confusion, thrown from his horse, and somewhat severely hurt, but Colonel Lugard, his chief of staff, assumed the command promptly and effectively. Shortly before daybreak the desultory firing ceased, and many have placed on record the almost tearful anxiety with which our men, prayed that the enemy might not have withdrawn before they should have a chance of "getting their own back." At last, the morning broke, and to the glee of all ranks the Persian Army, under the Shooja-ool-moolk, its commander, was descried "in position," drawn up in line, "its right upon the walled village of Khooshab, its left resting on a hamlet with a round fortalice tower."

As early as possible our artillery were moved up to the front, and murderous volleys were loosed upon the enemy's right, while our infantry were getting into line.

One account says:—

All night long, our cavalry had lain down beside their horses, watching the glare of the Persian guns, and wondering whether they would have an opportunity to seize them as trophies.

The opportunity came soon enough. Whether from impatience or some mistaken order, before the infantry could get within musket-shot, our horsemen hurled themselves upon the right wing, and cut their way clean through the Persian force with awful slaughter, and without the assistance of a shot from our infantry, soon had it in full retreat.

The left wing of the enemy was thunderstruck. Without pausing for an instant, they fell back, the two wings thus gradually converging until they became a disordered stream of fugitive infantry, without sufficient discipline to rally, yet without sufficient sense to separate from one another, and so avoid, to some extent, the fearful fire with which our artillery now plied them.

The eighteen guns opened with a roar, and the carnage began. For three long miles dozens of the wretched Persians dropped in their tracks, plied alternately by horse artillery and cavalry, and their retreat became almost a massacre.

Indeed, in one instance, since it was found that many of the wounded fired upon our men after their lives had been spared, a group of forty fugitives were cut down to a man, though making signs of wishing to surrender. Again and again throughout the Persian campaign did the enemy behave in this treacherous manner, and the giving of quarter became a precarious leniency.

By eleven o'clock the fight and pursuit alike were at an end, and the Battle of Khooshab was won.

The British loss was nearly a hundred killed and wounded; the Persians left seven hundred dead upon the far-extending field. Immense quantities of arms and ammunition fell into our hands, and high praise was bestowed by Sir James Outram on all ranks at the highly satisfactory conclusion of the fight.

After a tedious march, during which they were much hampered by rain, darkness, almost impassable country, and, in one instance, by the mistaken leading of a native guide, our army returned to Bushire, and for several days a well-earned rest was indulged in. Heavy rains fell during these days of waiting, but, when the weather was fine, cricket and occasional race meetings kept up the spirits of our men in camp, and another brush with the enemy was the dearest wish of every one of our gallant soldiers, white and coloured alike.

At this time General Havelock, destined to win fame in India, arrived and took command of the 2nd Division.

Meanwhile, rumours that the enemy was gathering in force at Mohammerah began to come to hand, and as this fort stands at the head of the Persian Gulf, some thirty hours north of Bushire, and commands the entrance to the Tigris and Euphrates, it was felt to be of great importance, and so preparations were soon on foot for its reduction.

In miserable weather, and hampered by sand-storms, our men erected five strong redoubts for the defence of Bushire, and here General Stalker was left in command, with two field batteries, the entire first division cavalry, some of the 64th and Highlanders, together with some native troops.

The remainder, to the number of 3,000, were embarked upon the transports and war vessels, and, under Sir James Outram himself, set sail for Mohammerah.

The 6th March saw the sailing of the sloop *Falkland* for the Euphrates, and the ships engaged in the expedition composed the sloop *Circe*, with the frigate steamers *Ajdaha*, *Feroze*, *Semiramis*, *Victoria*, and *Assaye*. Transports were numerous, and included the *Kingston* and *Bridge of the Sea*. These, together with the steamers *Pottinger* and *Pioneer*, newly arrived from India, with a fresh troop of horse artillery and the Scinde Horse, made up the fleet.

Mohammerah lies on the north side of the River Kanin, close to its junction with the Shat-ul-Arab, a branch of the Euphrates, and is about thirty miles from the sea. For a quarter of a mile from the river's mouth strong earthworks lined with artillery and musketry guarded its approach.

Now, while the left bank of the Shat-ul-Arab belongs to Persia, the right, for sixty miles, is Turkish territory, and accordingly the attitude of Turkey was somewhat apprehensively regarded, since a hostile demonstration in the river might be regarded by that Power as an infringement of the laws of neutrality. Accordingly, no time was lost so that Mohammerah might be taken before Turkey could have time to interfere. In point of fact, several Turks were killed in the engagement, the inhabitants of the Turkish territory crowding to the river's banks to watch the issue of the fight.

By the 8th, most of the vessels had arrived in the mouth of the Euphrates, and the remainder were expected in the course of the next few days. A tedious wait followed, but by the 17th, Sir James Outram, with the remainder of the force, arrived in the river, and an advance was hourly expected.

Sir James brought bad news. In a fit of mental derangement, both General Stalker and Captain Ethersay, the commodore of the Indian squadron serving in the Persian Gulf, had died by their own hands at Bushire, and considerable gloom was cast over the fleet by these sad events.

Captain Hunt says:—

No cause, save over-anxiety and an oppressive sense of their respective responsibilities could be assigned as a reason for their rash acts.

On the 24th, all vessels were assembled at the rendezvous, some three miles below the enemy's fortifications; a day was spent in transhipping troops into rafts and light-draught vessels, and at daybreak on the 26th the bombardment of Mohammerah began.

The first shot proved highly successful, killing eleven of the enemy, who, it was afterwards ascertained, were at their prayers; and soon after this the action became general.

It is impossible to resist once more quoting Captain Hunt:—

The morning being very clear, with just sufficient breeze to prevent the smoke from collecting, a more beautiful scene than was then presented can scarcely be imagined. The ships, with ensigns flying from every masthead, seemed decked for a holiday; the river glittering in the early sunlight, its dark date-fringed banks contrasting most effectively with the white canvas of the Falkland, which had loosened sails to get into closer action; the sulky-looking batteries just visible through the grey fleecy cloud which enveloped them; and groups of brightly-dressed horsemen flitting at intervals between the trees, formed altogether a picture from which even the excitement of a heavy cannonade could not divert the attention.

At the end of three hours the Persian fire slackened, and the order for the disembarkation of the troops, at a point selected above the batteries, went forth. A few musket shots alone opposed the landing, and by two o'clock the entire force was ashore and an advance made.

By this time the fire of the Persian forts was silenced, one of the final shells of our ships blowing up the enemy's grand magazine.

Forward now moved the compact scarlet lines to where the enemy's force under the Shah Zadeh in person were drawn up to defend their camp on the left rear of the town of Mohammerah, and a desperate fight appeared about to open. Suddenly, almost as if by magic, the force disappeared.

Paralysed by our fire, particularly by the size of the 68-pounder shots, and fearing awful consequences, the *Shah's* terrible army turned and ran, and though the pursuit was engaged in for three or four miles, only a straggler or two was cut off. At night our cavalry returned, and reported that the enemy, at a distance of eleven miles, was still in full retreat.

Our troops bivouacked in line of battle, but such caution proved to be superfluous, and on the morning of the 27th the British Army took possession of Mohammerah.

Stores of grain and ammunition, 18 handsome brass guns in good working order, arms of all kinds, and tents fell into our hands, for a total loss of 10 killed, with one officer, Lieutenant Harris of the Indian navy, and 30 wounded. The Persians had at least 300 killed, while many prisoners were taken.

These latter received every kindness, but for a long time were suspicious of their captors, expecting a fate which would probably have overtaken any of our brave fellows who might have fallen into Persian hands. Fortunately, such a contingency had not to be faced.

The town of Mohammerah, once a place of importance, was found to be a filthy collection of mud huts, and apart from its fortifications (where the guns had been admirably served, some of our ships suffering severely as a result), was found to be of little practical use. The moral effect of such a victory was enormous.

A small expedition under Captain Rennie was despatched up the Kanin River to reconnoitre, while the general fortified Mohammerah to the best of his ability before deciding upon a further plan of campaign.

By the 4th April, Captain Rennie's expedition returned, and reported having seen the Persian Army at Ahway. After a few shots, he had captured the town, together with immense stores of grain and powder, the Persian Army again retreating with little show of fight. These operations were about to be turned to advantage by the commander-in-chief when a despatch was received announcing that peace with Persia, had been concluded at Paris.

Accordingly, operations were at once commenced for evacuating Mohammerah, though the disappointment to all ranks was keen. By the end of May the evacuation was complete, though Bushire was held till October, when it was handed back to the Persians.

Apart from prestige, an important factor in Eastern politics, the Persian campaign of '56 and '57 may be said to have been of little practical use, but one good result accruing must not be overlooked. It prepared some, at any rate, of our troops for the tremendous struggle which was even then brewing in India.

CHAPTER 16

The Battles at Delhi: 1857

The Indian Mutiny had really its outbreak at Delhi, to which place the mutineers fled when they had taken the fatal step which was to bring death to so many, and which was to weld the Indian Empire closer to Britain.

The imperial city of Delhi was destined to play an important part in the mutiny, and early in May, 1857, the mutineers, inflamed with preliminary successes and inspired by a religious frenzy, entered Delhi. Mr. Simon Frazer, the Commissioner, tried to stem the tide by closing the seven gates of the city, but his orders were tardily obeyed, and the mutineers poured into the city, carrying havoc wherever they went. The bungalows in the Durya Gunge were soon in flames, and every European was slaughtered.

No white man or woman could venture forth and hope to return alive, for the rebel soldiers, having tasted blood, were determined to have their appetites whetted. Mr. Frazer ventured out in his buggy to the residence of the Delhi princes, but was seized, and after a desperate struggle was hacked to pieces. His head was struck off, and, horrible to relate, was carried through the streets in barbarous triumph.

Terrible were the tragedies enacted within the walls, and the hapless Europeans calmly waited death, for they knew that they would receive no mercy. At the palace fort the rebels asked to see Captain Douglas, who commanded the guard, and on that brave officer appearing, he was shot down ere he could utter a word. In their hunt for victims, they ascended to the murdered officer's quarters, and found there the chaplain of the station, Rev. Mr. Jennings, and his daughter, who had lately arrived from England to be married. They were deaf to her agonising cries and prayers for mercy, and butchered her father before her eyes. After subjecting the poor girl to awful indignities, they hacked her to pieces.

The Delhi arsenal, was at the time of the outbreak the largest in India, and it was well that Britain had brave and capable officers at this quarter. The powder magazine was included in the arsenal, although there was another at the cantonments about two miles from the walls of the city, where three battalions of Bengal infantry were posted. The mutineers intended to attack this point (the arsenal), and Sir T. Metcalfe on the morning that the insurgents initiated the attack closed up the gate at the bridge. He did not suspect that the princes and members of the royal family were hand-in-glove with the mutineers, but his eyes were opened when he saw the rebels march through the palace, which could only have been done through the complicity of the princes.

There were only six Britons to defend the arsenal, in charge of sullen and stubborn men whom they dreaded to trust. Guns were posted at every point where attack was possible, and right nobly did the gallant half-dozen prepare to sell their lives dearly in defence of the position. The mutineers were now having the full support of the natives of Delhi, and armed guards came boldly to the arsenal, and demanded its surrender in the name of the King of Delhi. This request was treated with the silent contempt which it deserved, and then, the King of Delhi showed his hand by declaring that he would send men with scaling ladders to scale the walls.

When these ladders did arrive, the native portion of the garrison availed themselves of this opportunity to desert their posts, and, swarming down the ladders, left the gallant six alone. Outside the howling mass of insurgents, waving their *tulwars* on high and calling upon the defenders to come out and be killed. Inside, every man of the six—Lieutenants Forrest and Willoughby, Sergeant Stewart, and Conductors Crow, Buckley, and Scully—were cool and calm at their respective post.

The enemy now began to appear on the top of the walls, and the garrison poured a deadly grape fire upon these customers until the ammunition became almost exhausted. The natives who had deserted the garrison had given valuable information to the rebels as to the position of the guns. Forrest and Buckley were firing and loading the guns as fast as they could, and while the unequal struggle lasted, they mowed down the closely-packed rebels. And this they did under a heavy musketry fire at forty yards' range. It was not until the last round that Buckley had his arm shot and Forrest received two balls in one of his hands. Willoughby had determined that the rebels would never secure the magazine and all its valuable store. A train of powder had been laid by Conductor Scully, and when all seemed lost the Lieutenant gave orders to blow up the magazine.

The fire rushed along the trains of powder, and then an awful crash and roar which seemed to split the earth and rend the vault of heaven told the rebels that they had been thwarted by the *Feringhee*. The whole magazine with its deadly contents was hurled into the air, and fell, burying hundreds of the rebels in the ruins.

Meanwhile the brave defenders had made a dash for liberty and reached the Cashmere gate. The brave Willoughby was captured while hiding in the jungle, and, after terrible torture, was mercifully put to death. Simultaneous with the attack upon the magazines, things were going hard, with the surviving Christian population. The infuriated cowards who glutted their appetite for blood by the massacre of helpless women and children, had gone too far to turn back, for they knew that if the *Feringhees* became victorious they would all perish. They broke into the bank, and Mr. Beresford, the manager, with his wife and five children, perished. They devised the torturing death of cutting their victims' throats slowly with broken glass, and it was in this cruel manner that the bank manager and his family were murdered.

All the public buildings and churches were plundered, and robbery and murder was rampant in the streets of the city. A *sepoy* when he takes service, makes a vow to remain true to his salt, *i.e.,* true to their employers. This vow was even more binding in the case of those who had sworn to serve the Queen of Britain, even with their lives, but we shall see how the crafty natives who wore the queen's uniform and her medals evaded their vow and yet, in their own opinion, remained true to their salt.

Colonel Ripley was despatched from the cantonments with the 54th Bengal Native Infantry, which had remained loyal, and the line of march lay towards the Cashmere gate. They obeyed their officers with alacrity, and marched boldly forward. Suddenly fifteen troopers of the rebel 3rd cavalry came dashing out to meet them, brandishing their blood-smeared swords. The treachery of the 54th was soon made apparent, for, on the approach of the *sowars* they wheeled to the side of the road and left their officers unguarded in the troopers' path.

The maniac mutineers dashed upon the bewildered officers and shot or cut them down. Colonel Ripley had his pistols with him, and shot two troopers before being killed. When the slaughter was complete, the bloodstained troopers dismounted, and, walking amongst the treacherous 54th, shook hands and complimented their fellow-villains on their action.

The brigadier at the cantonments had now only the 38th and 74th. to fall back upon, both native regiments, in whose fidelity he could put little trust. At all events he formed them into line, posting the 38th on the road that led to the Cashmere gate. As long as possible news of the mutiny of the 54th was kept from the other regiments, but when at last they heard it, they showed evident symptoms of mutiny. When, the awful crash of the exploded magazine fell upon their ears, the outburst came. "*Deen! Deen!*" they shouted, signifying "Faith!" and rushed to their arms, which had been piled. They seized the guns, shot the *commandant's* horse, and were soon in a state of complete insubordination.

The first regard of British officers and men in time of danger, whether it be on sea or land, is for the women and children, and now that the *sepoys* had shown themselves in their true colours, it was absolutely imperative, if the women and children were to be saved from terrible torture, that they should be removed to either Meerut or Kurnool, cities which were meanwhile loyal and unaffected. Brigadier Metcalfe sounded the retire, and those who could find conveyances were fortunate, as in most cases the native drivers had bolted with the horses and vehicles.

In the guard-house at the Cashmere gate a number of women and children, along with several officers, were huddled. Major Abbott, who was in charge, made the attempt to get the helpless females to the shelter of the cantonments, and ordered them to be placed on the gun carriages. The rebel *sepoys* opened a murderous fire on the carriages, and the ground was soon strewn with the dead and wounded. Several reached the shelter of Brigadier Metcalfe's house, from whence they were conducted to the River Jumna, where they were allowed to make their escape as best they could.

We need not dwell upon the harrowing details of the adventures of those who escaped. They wandered about the jungle, starving and bruised. Delicately-nurtured women clinging to their babes went raving mad, and many perished. The villagers were every whit as brutal and cruel as the rebel soldiery, and men boasted publicly of outraging white women and then cutting off their breasts. It makes one's blood boil to think of the awful indignities, the almost incredible tortures, and the slow lingering death which was the fate of our innocent and helpless women and children.

Certain nations accused us of wanton cruelty in the slaying of the rebels at the time when the hand of retribution, guided by Sir Colin Campbell, fell upon the inhuman monsters who had weltered and gloried in the shedding of Christian blood. Could the stab of the bayonet, blowing from the cannon's mouth or death by hanging ever atone for the fearful sufferings of the pure and innocent? In our humanity we scorned to devise new tortures or have recourse to those of the Inquisition to avenge the massacre of the Christian women who had been outraged and done to death. If those who escaped to the jungle suffered untold agony, it was nothing to that which the women who remained in Delhi had to undergo. An officer who had to be an unwilling witness of many of the scenes tells the following bloodcurdling story:—

The *sepoys* took forty-eight females, most of them girls from ten to fourteen, many delicately nurtured ladies, and kept them for the base purposes of the heads of the insurrection for a whole week. At the end of that time, they made them strip themselves, and gave them up to the lowest of the people to abuse in broad daylight in the streets of Delhi. They then commenced the work of torturing them to death, cutting off their breasts, fingers, and noses. One lady was three days in dying. They flayed the face of another lady, and made her walk naked through the streets.

A number of officers, women, and children sought refuge in a mosque, where they were without food and water for several days. The men could have endured the hunger and thirst, but the suffering of the women and little children was intense. On the fourth day they treated with the *sepoys*, who on their oath swore to spare their lives and take them before the king. The men laid down their arms that they might get water for the suffering ones, and the whole party quitted the shelter of the mosque. They were instantly seized, and every one killed, eight officers, eight ladies, and eleven children perishing. The children were swung by the heels, and their brains dashed out in, the presence of the parents.

On every side were traces of murder and pillage, and it is said that even greater ferocity, if that were possible, was used at Delhi than by the great assassin Nana Sahib at Cawnpore. Certainly, the atrocities practised are unequalled in barbarity and cruelty, and coming from men who had broken our bread and eaten our salt, they demanded

DELHI, 1857

the most condign punishment. Delhi was now in full possession of the mutineers, and this ancient city, with its hundred mosques and minarets, seemed lost to the British Empire, for the 200,000 inhabitants were in no way reluctant to accept the change in government.

The king, seeing that Fortune had so far smiled on the insurgents, put himself at the head of the new movement. This crafty monarch, whose kingdom lay within the walls of the city, had a love of pomp and panoply, and no doubt delighted his followers by a State procession through the city to the palace of the Moguls. This is an immense edifice of more than a mile in circumference. The wall which surrounds it is over thirty feet in height, and besides serving as a kingly residence, it thus stands as a gigantic fortress.

The princes of the royal house were also concerned in the spread of the mutiny, Prince Mirza Mogul being commander-in-chief of the army, and his brother Mirza Abubeker, general of the cavalry. Although they had foully murdered many of their officers, the *sepoys*, to give them credit, did not run amok altogether, but put themselves under the command of native officers of inferior rank, who were now given high commands. They also knew that Britain would not let them hold undisturbed possession of the town, so they set about preparing defences in order to withstand a siege. Heavy guns were mounted on the bastions, and the guards were strengthened at the seven gates.

The mutiny was not long in spreading throughout the provinces, and regiment after regiment rose in insurrection, and either murdered their officers or fled to Delhi. From every part, tidings came to Agra of a general rising, and it was not safe for any British officer to place himself at the head of any native regiment. The *sepoys* would swear undying fidelity at one moment, and the next might be either butchering their officers or on the road to join the main band of rebels at Delhi. Will our men be faithful? was the question many an officer had to put to himself, for they were not to be trusted, despite all their vows.

The British regiments, manned and officered by Europeans, had to pass through many perils, and undoubtedly, they did good service in punishing the flying rebels. They shot and bayonetted the *sepoys* who had mutinied, and only took prisoner those of higher caste, and those who had set themselves up in the leadership of the work of mutiny. These rascals were reserved for another fate, either at the hands of the hangman, or, greater punishment still in the eyes of a true believer blown from the cannon's mouth.

This form of punishment may have been brutal, but it was thoroughly deserved, and the swift death cannot be likened to the lingering tortures to which the women and children of our own flesh and blood had to submit. As this method of punishment became common as the mutiny proceeded, a description of the scene at an execution may be of interest:—

Three sides of a hollow square facing inwards was formed. On the fourth side of the square were drawn up the guns, ten 9-pounders, which were to be used for the execution. The prisoners, under a strong European guard, were then marched into the square, their crimes and sentences read aloud to them and at the head of each regiment; they were then marched round the square and up to the guns. The first ten were picked out, their eyes bandaged, and they were bound to the guns, with their backs against the muzzles and their arms fastened backwards to the wheels. The port fires were lighted, and at a signal from the artillery major the guns were fired.

It was a horrid sight that then met the eye. A regular shower of human fragments—of heads, arms, and legs—appeared in the air, whirling through the smoke; and when that cleared away, these fragments lying on the ground—fragments of Hindoos and of Mussulmans mixed together—were all that remained of those ten mutineers. Three times more this was repeated; but so great is the disgust we all feel for the atrocities committed by the rebels, that we had no room in our hearts for any feeling of pity. Perfect callousness was depicted on, every European face; a look of grim satisfaction could even be seen in the countenances of the gunners serving the guns. But far different was the effect on the native portion of the spectators. Their black faces grew ghastly pale as they gazed breathlessly at the awful spectacle.

You must know that this is really the only form in which death has any terror for a native. If he is hanged or shot, he knows that his friends or relatives will be allowed to claim his body and will give him the funeral rites required by his religion; if a Hindoo, that his body will be burned with all due ceremonies, and if a Mussulman, that his remains will be secretly interred, as directed in the *Koran*. But if sentenced to death in this form, he knows that his body will be blown into a thousand pieces, and that it will be altogether impossible for his relatives, however devoted to him, to be sure of picking up all the fragments of his own particular body; and the thought that perhaps a limb of some-one of a different religion to himself might possibly be burned or buried with the remainder of his own body, is agony to him. But notwithstanding this, it was impossible for the mutineers' direst hater not to feel some degree of admiration for the way in which they met their deaths. Nothing in their lives became them like the leaving of them. Of the whole party, only two showed any signs of fear, and they were bitterly reproached by the others for so disgracing their race. They certainly died like men. After the first ten had been disposed of, the next batch, who had been looking on all the time, walked up to the guns quite calmly and unfalteringly, and allowed themselves to be blindfolded and tied up without moving a muscle or showing the slightest sign of fear or even concern.

The army of vengeance which was to stamp out the mutiny and punish the mutineers, was pushing on from Umballa. The great vortex of the mutiny was at Delhi, and the rebels had such excellent fortifica-tions and were so well armed and provisioned, that a prolonged siege was anticipated. There were many princes with large bands of followers who as yet had taken no part on either side. They were wise as Solo-mon in their judgment, for they deferred taking the great step until they saw how the game was to go. These princes and chiefs of the Del-hi provinces were loyal enough, but, like the rebel *sepoys*, they would turn round and cut our throats if it was to profit them in any way.

Holkar and Scindia had already sent their contingents, to Agra for service under the British flag, and now the *rajahs* of Jheend and Putti-ala, two powerful chiefs, sent well-drilled horsemen, and the Rajah of Bhurtpur gave his specially-trained bodyguard. These men were good fighters, and would remain loyal and true to their salt as long as their *rajah* willed. General Barnard, who was in command of the troops, pushed on as fast as he could to Delhi, and sent Brigadier Wilson with an advance guard to clear a path.

The gallant brigadier came up with the enemy at a place known as Ghazee-ood-deen-nugger on the 30th of May, and distant about 15 miles from Delhi. The rebels were present in large numbers, and had some heavy guns to which they trusted in keeping their position. Wil-son at once saw that the small iron suspension bridge over the River Hindon would form a key to his own attack, and two companies of the 60th Rifles were told off to keep the bridge at all hazards, while a detachment of the 6th Dragoon Guards, with four guns, went along the riverside to turn the enemy's flank.

The 60th at the bridge were exposed to a heavy fire from the insurgents' guns, and had to be reinforced. It was plainly evident that the rebels were aware that if they lost this position an important point to the capture of the city would be gained. They handled their guns with great skill, but when the 60th dashed among them with the bayonet they blanched, wavered, and turned tail, leaving the guns in the hands of the Rifles.

"Remember the ladies! remember the babies!" was the battle-cry of the 60th, as they flashed on with gleaming bayonets, and many a mother and many a child were amply avenged in the terrible slaughter they wrought.

Fleeing from the infuriated and victorious troops, the *sepoys* fled helter-skelter towards Delhi, leaving their guns and hundreds of dead and dying on the field. The Carbineers, who added to the death-toll in the course of the pursuit, chased the fleeing horde to within a few miles of the city. Yet they were not cowed, for, despite the lesson they had received, they were back in greater numbers to the banks of the Hindon the following day. They opened fire with their muskets and big guns, and for two hours there was nothing heard but the boom of the guns and the rattle of musketry. The rebel fire began to slacken, and it was now the time for close combat.

Once again, the 60th defiled across the bridge, with the 6th Dragoon Guards as support. Alternately firing and charging, the British rushed the rising ground, on which the rebels were posted, and once again the mutineers had to fly to the sheltering walls of Delhi. Our men were too fagged out to pursue, but there was not an inch of fight in the fleeing mass, and many of them cast their swords and guns away in their panic.

The British burned a village which afforded shelter for the enemy, and were content to take a well-won rest. General Barnard was daily expected, and the brigadier calmly waited, undisturbed by the faint-hearted mutineers, until such time as the general would order a grand advance upon the Imperial City.

Akbar Fort, Allahabad

CHAPTER 17

The Battles at Delhi (continued): 1857

The army of vengeance was steadily closing upon Delhi, and the plans of Sir Henry Barnard as to the junctions of his force were attended with success. Major-General Reed, who had fought at Waterloo, arrived at Alleepore, situated about one day's march from Delhi, while Brigadier Wilson's troops from the Meerut provinces had joined Sir Henry Barnard, so that the investing force was as complete as could be expected.

As its composition is important, the different details of the force may be interesting, and are as follows:—

Four horse artillery guns of the 1st Brigade, the 2nd and 3rd troops of the 3rd Brigade, three companies of foot artillery, No. 14 horse field battery, a detachment of artillery recruits, a detachment of sappers and miners, H.M. 9th Lancers and 6th Dragoon Guards, six companies of the 60th Rifles, nine companies of H.M. 75th regiment, 1st and 2nd Bengal Fusiliers, and the Sirmoor battalion of Ghoorkas.

The city round which the conflict now centred deserves some little description, not, only for its historic associations, but its immense importance as a British stronghold. It is a huge conglomeration of houses, mosques, fortresses, and temples surrounded by strongly-fortified walls. It lies in the midst of a sandy plain, on a plateau close to the River Jumna. Its streets are wide and handsome, especially the "street of silver," through which runs an aqueduct shaded by overhanging palms. The mosques are all of magnificent appearance, but the most stately and ornate is the huge snow-white marble edifice built by Shah Johan, with its towering minarets and beautiful sculpture. Again, if we go outside the city walls through any of the seven gates, we come upon the remains of the great buildings of other days.

The present-day Delhi is modern to a degree, and when we gaze upon the ruins of gigantic buildings, of masques and temples, we have an idea of the Delhi of centuries ago. We have the mausoleums of the Emperors Homaion Mahomed Shah and Jehanara, but the commanding feature is the towering Kootub Minar, which was built in 1206, and is covered over with extracts from the Koran, the walls rising to a height of about 240 feet, terminating in a majestic cupola. Such was the general appearance of the city which had passed into the hands of mutineers, and naturally the British leaders were anxious to regain, it.

Inside the city, the mutineers, after their first excess of brutality, and no doubt through a scarcity of victims, must have thought of the retribution that would surely follow. To give them credit, they were not lawless or idle, but obeyed the mandates of their chosen leaders. Military discipline and order were maintained, and men who had occupied very subordinate positions in the employ of Britain, found promotion easy and rapid in the service of the King of Delhi. Yet the townspeople were downtrodden by the savage soldiery, and the town was daily the scene of great disorder.

The *sepoys* looted in every direction, and stuffed their pockets full to overflowing, in fact in many cases they could not walk, so laden were, they with coin and treasure. Had Sir Henry Barnard made a dash upon the city when he first gathered together his forces, it is quite possible that, Delhi would have fallen into our hands, because the townspeople were so discontented that they would have turned against the rebels. However, the British leader was not apparently aware of this situation, and preferred to rest his troops and mature his plans for the taking of the city.

Now the defences of Delhi were of a formidable character, having been strengthened by officers and men of the B Fusiliers several years previous, and the rebels kept a double watch upon the bastions and Martello towers.

After resting his troops sufficiently, Sir Henry gave orders to the effect that an advance was premeditated, and at midnight on the 8th of June the combined Umballa and Meerut force started to march upon the city. After marching for about three miles without meeting any opposition, the British troops were suddenly confronted by a strong rebel force with a dozen heavy guns, which had been placed in a strong position. In the glimmering light of the morning, the rebels opened deadly fire upon the British lines, and did much execution, our lighter guns being unable to cope with, the heavier ordnance the enemy. Men were falling, and every life was precious, something had to be done.

THE STORMING OF DELHI

"Charge and carry the guns!" cried Sir Henry, and like hounds released from the leash the men of the 75th—that gallant Stirlingshire regiment—bounded forward to death or glory. Through a storm of musketry they dashed, and sprang at the gunners with glittering bayonets. The *sepoys* turned tail and fled, the guns were ours, and the brave Scotsmen paused to regain breath. The rebels had retired to a second position, where they had a line of defence; at the Flagstaff Tower. They fought like men who fight when they feel the halter round their necks, but they reeled before the bayonet, and were soon in full stampede towards the city, to tell their comrades that the *Feringhees* had come to put them to death.

Our men had gained the old Delhi cantonments, but when they marched in, what a different place it was to that which had been so well garrisoned but a few months previous! Only the blackened walls remained, and all was desolation. Fragments of furniture, scraps of books, clothing, and shreds of women's dresses lay about. The soldiers took one look upon the desolate scene, and looking, understood, for they turned their eyes to Delhi and ground their teeth. They knew what the torn and bloodstained garments signified, and although they said no word there was a gleam in their eyes which betokened no good for the rebels when they had them, at the point of the bayonet. They were not hurried in their vengeance, but pitched their camps to await further reinforcements.

The enemy, seeing that the British did not follow up their early success, grew bolder, and made frequent sallies, but their skirmishing amongst the ruins and tombs of the Delhi of a day that was dead was ineffective, and did little harm to the troops at the cantonment. But the British were not idle, for three batteries played on the city day and night. The guns must have done considerable damage to the city, for the mutineers turned a number of guns upon this position. It was a stoutly-built brick house, and withstood the rebel fire, while the daily attacks of the mutineers upon the battery were easily repulsed by the defending force, which consisted of the Guides, the Sirmoor battalion, and three companies of the 60th Rifles.

In one of these sorties brave young Lieutenant Battye of the Guides received a terrible wound in the stomach from a cannon shot. He survived for a day, and ere he died he smiled to a comrade who came to see him, and quoted the old tag—"Well, old fellow, '*dulce et decorum est pro patria mori*' ('it is sweet and proper to die for one's country'); you see it's my case," and then he passed away.

The Guides, who were led by their commander, Captain Daly, came into contact with the mutineers, who sniped at them from behind rocks. They took careful cover, and the Guides could not get a shot at them. The rebels were good marksmen, and several of the Guides fell. Daly and another officer drew their swords and rushed up the rocks. They were followed by their men, and although the *sepoys* made strenuous efforts to keep their position the sword and bayonet soon demoralised them.

It was on the 12th of June that the mutineers became most dangerous, and suffered the severest chastisement; yet administered. They came out of the city in great numbers, and commenced to fire upon the Ghoorkas, until the 2nd Bengal Fusiliers came up to the post and drove them back from the place. The force pushed home the blow, but as they were unsupported, they had to retire, leaving their leader, Major Jackson, dead behind them. The rebels returned, and the 60th regiment, who had taken up a position in Hindoo Rao's house, which commanded a fine situation, had a very hard day's fighting. The Scotsmen and the fierce little Ghoorkas fought with hordes of rebels, who, despite severe losses, returned to the attack persistently, and displayed much courage.

The Welsh Fusiliers' left wing, now under the command of Welshman, had again taken possession of the *Subzee Mundee*, or vegetable market, and cleared the streets. Four times did the enemy return to the attack, and as often were they repulsed. The heat was terrible, and our men were fairly exhausted with the heavy fighting. The right wing of the fusiliers, under Dennis, were also busily engaged with the enemy, and after driving them back citywards and killing a large number in a *serai*, they were done up, and returned to the shelter of the Hindoo Rao.

To give some idea of the terrible heat, it may be mentioned that the musket barrels and bayonet blades grew warm in the hands of the soldiers. Yet the fight never slackened, and the enemy, no doubt aware that our troops must become tired, kept up an attack all along the line. A large company of the 2nd Bengal Fusiliers, who had marched twenty-three miles that morning and had gone into battle with nothing to eat, were completely done up, having to take shelter behind some rocks, while the Ghoorkas kept the mutineers at a respectful distance. The rebels had two pieces of cannon playing on the British line, but the fusiliers and Sikhs charged and gained complete possession of the *Subzee Mundee*, driving the rebels away.

The greatest slaughter of the enemy took place at a *serai*, which is really a baiting-place for travellers. About a hundred rebels took shelter in this place, and no doubt felt secure behind the lofty walls. The 60th Rifles heard of their hiding-place, and rushing at the gates burst them open and entered. Then ensued a scene of carnage, for not a rebel was spared, the Scotsmen driving home the bayonet so fiercely that in many cases their weapons were twisted and bent.

The British troops were now masters of the field, and preparations were made for the mortars to be put into position to shell Delhi. A discovery was then made that caused consternation in the camp— the fuses had been left behind at Umballa. This was most regrettable, as no doubt Sir Henry would have followed up the shelling with a general attack. The commanding officers did not show much energy, and those in a position to judge declare that chance after chance was thrown away of at least strengthening the British hold upon Delhi. The troops on the other hand, however, deserved rest, and Sir Henry may have acted on the more careful plan of harbouring the strength of his troops and keeping them fresh for a future attack.

There can be no doubt, however, that the rebels gained courage by this apathy, and as they were strengthened by a number of rebellious regiments, notably the 4th Lancers and the 60th Bengal Infantry, they became even bolder, and harried the British to an extraordinary extent. They were fighting for their lives, and so desperately did they attack our weakened soldiers that if it had not been for a piece of splendid strategy by the officer in charge of the outposts, they might have defeated our troops or at least captured the guns.

The enemy had made this daring and desperate attack on the 15th of June, and had met with much success. The officer of the outposts knew that the rebels recognised our bugle-calls and understood them as well as our own men, so he determined to draw them into a trap. Dusk had now settled over the scene, and presently the bugles rang out the "Retire." The mutineers heard the blast, and in a confused mob, numbering thousands, they advanced tumultuously to pursue the retreating British. Their rush was suddenly checked, however, for when the mutineers were about thirty yards from the waiting British outposts the gallant leader gave the order to charge, and soon the dreaded bayonet was working havoc in the serried hordes, who lost heart and retired in confusion to their position.

The enemy now occupied their attention by forming a battery of heavy guns which rendered the British position at the house of

Hindoo Rao quite untenable. The whole force was now concentrated to checkmate this rebel move, and, marching upon the battery in two columns, our men drove the enemy back, won the guns and killed a large number of rebels, hemming about fifty into a corner, where they were shot down.

The town batteries, however, were still arrayed against us, five in number; a large one on the left of the Cashmere gate, a second at the gate itself, a third at the Moree gate, a fourth at the Ajmere gate, and the fifth on the city walls. These batteries were sweeping the British positions to the extent of over two miles, and they did great damage to our camp. We had three batteries, one at Hindoo Rao, another at the Observatory, and a third at the Jumna Musjid. On the 19th the rebels made another determined attack, and attempted to get to the rear of the British position.

Brigadier Hope Grant, with the 9th Lancers and six pieces of cannon, advanced to circumvent the enemy, but were assailed by a heavy fire of grape when they had reached the Ochterliny gardens, which lie near the cantonments. Grant's guns vigorously replied, and his force was at once reinforced, the attack becoming general. The rebels were fighting with determination, and the British flank was nearly turned, two of our guns being in danger of capture. With brave charges, however, the tide of battle turned, and the rebels fell back, enabling us to take the guns to a place of safety. The 9th Lancers, *Carbineers*, and the Guides were hotly engaged on the right flank, supporting the batteries of Majors Turner and Tombs.

The ground was not at all suitable for a pitched battle, being of a very broken character, and the fight developed into a series of skirmishes. Our leadership was muddled, and at one time the cavalry, artillery, and infantry were all mixed up, and had it not been for the individual energy of the commanding officers of the various regiments, the confusion might have been attended with serious consequences. Sir Henry Barnard seemed incapable of proceeding upon a preconcerted plan, and the different officers were left to adopt whatever tactics they thought fit.

The enemy was strongly posted, and their fire was well directed, our loss being every whit as heavy as that which we inflicted. Darkness came on, and, instead of retiring to the camp, the troops were ordered to fight on. Needless to say, the confusion became worse, and if the enemy had come to know of the terrible position of our troops and charged, the total rout of our men must have been inevitable. When at last the order came to retire, many of our cannon, had to be left on the field until morning, along with the killed and wounded. Among the former was the gallant Colonel Yule of the 9th Lancers, who lay upon the field with four of his men around him. Both thighs had been broken, a ball had passed through his brain, and his throat had been cut .

It was a miserable fate for such a gallant officer, who had passed with glory through many a bloody field. The rebels also lost a great number in killed and wounded, but they were so strong that the sacrifice of a few hundred lives made little difference of their numerical strength. Our brave soldiers never lost heart, although they felt that they were badly led, not by their own officers, but by the general in command.

The anniversary of the Battle of Plassey (23rd June) came round, and as it was a festival for both Mohammedans and Hindoos alike, being the first day of the new moon, they became even more fanatical, making a furious attack upon our outposts. It is said that every man in Delhi capable of bearing arms came out to exterminate the *Feringhees*, but as the British had taken the precaution of blowing up two bridges, they could not get their artillery forward. The army opposed to our battered but determined troops was an immense one, and if the confusion of the previous attack had prevailed, our force would have been swamped.

From sunset to sunrise the battle raged, and fierce were the rebel attacks, only to be met with dogged resistance by our men. Repulsed again and again, the rebels grew less determined, and slackened perceptibly, while the British, advancing, drove the enemy back to the city, leaving the field littered with the dead and dying. Our loss was also severe, and thus was the anniversary of Clive's victory celebrated before the walls of Delhi.

It would have been almost impossible now for Barnard to take Delhi with the attenuated force at his disposal, and valuable time was thus lost. He was reinforced by about 500 Europeans, which made up the entire force to 3,000 British troops, with three native corps of 600 bayonets each, consisting of the Ghoorkas, Guides, and a Sikh battalion. Continually harassed by the enemy, who were fighting desperately to retain their advantage, our troops lay before Delhi having achieved but scant success, and having little idea of any regular plan. Sir Henry's apathy cannot be accounted for, unless it was due to the fact that he was content to wait until fortune made an opening for him; but he might have waited long enough for that.

The mutiny had by this time spread with alarming rapidity, and all over India, the *sepoys*, inflamed with the reports of rebel successes, murdered their officers and joined the mutineers. There can be no doubt that the resistance of the rebels at Delhi encouraged the mutineers at other points, and while Barnard's force was lying under the very walls of the ancient capital, the rebels were being daily reinforced by numerous bands of mutineers who made Delhi their Mecca.

Rain fell heavily in July, but still our troops were inactive, beyond repulsing occasional sallies by the enemy. Sir Henry was engaged in forming a plan whereby he could gain the city with the least loss of life, but his officers were quite convinced that the city would only be won by a vigorous attack at different gates.

The enemy kept well within the walls, apparently not desirous of engaging the *Feringhees* in the open. On the 9th of July they made a daring sally, and a body of their cavalry got to the rear of our position through the treachery of a picket of the 9th Irregular Horse. They gained no advantage, being driven off' with severe loss. An incident of this skirmish is worthy of mention. Lieutenant Hills of the Horse Artillery, escorted by 80 of the 6th Carbineers, came suddenly upon a troop of about 120 *sowars*. A panic ensued amongst his escort, who retired, leaving the guns limbered and useless to Hills.

He confronted the enemy, shot two, and unhorsed a third by throwing his pistol at the rebel's head. He was charged by another two of the enemy, and, although thrown to the ground, he felled one of his adversaries before he was cut down from behind. Major Tombs, who was hurrying to his comrade's assistance only arrived in time to shoot the assailant, and running another through the body, he bore off his bleeding comrade. The mutineers lost heavily in this skirmish, but the British also sustained considerable loss. For a few days the enemy remained singularly quiet, and as yet there was no appearance of an aggressive movement on our part.

The rebels had not done with us, however, as on the 14th they poured out of the city about 10,000 strong, and made a furious onslaught upon our right flank. They poured in a murderous fire, which was instantly replied to. The attack and repulse lasted in skirmishing affrays for about three hours, when the enemy seemed to realise that they had had enough of it, and, leaving their dead and wounded behind, they made off as fast as they could to their place of refuge behind the city walls. Our soldiers, eager for the fray, and no doubt throwing their usual caution to the winds, kept up the pursuit until they came up close to the walk. They rushed into a perfect hail of musket balls and grape shot, and before they came to their senses and obeyed the bugles, which were sounding the recall, 16 officers and 230 men were placed on the wounded list, a number succumbing to their wounds.

This was a foolhardy action, involving a needless loss of life, but, done as it was in the heat of battle, it showed the fearlessness of the British troops, and no doubt had its effect upon the miscreants in the city.

Further attacks were made on the 18th and 23rd, but both were firmly met, and considerable chastisement meted out to the bold rebels. Although Sir Henry Barnard was in supreme charge, the active command rested with General Reed, whose health now broke down, necessitating his retiral to the hills. The operations before Delhi were now entrusted to, and ably conducted by, Brigadier Wilson of the Bengal Artillery, a zealous and active officer.

On the last day of July, the enemy made another attempt to break our lines, and appeared in force at the Cashmere and Ajmere gates. One column got a couple of guns into position, and played on the Mosque and our central battery, while the other endeavoured to get to the rear of the camp, but being unable to cross the canal they returned to the city. It was evidently a well-planned attack, for the guns on the walls gave them a lot of assistance through a constant fire on our position, which was rather out of range.

All through the night the rebels kept up an incessant fire upon our outposts, while their bugles were heard continually sounding the advance, yet no advance came. Frantically the leaders rushed about, shouting "*Chulo chai! chulo!*" ("Come on, brother! come on!") but no one seemed willing to answer the call.

The incessant boom of the gun continued until the 2nd August, but not much damage was done to our earthworks and batteries. The rebels seemed to be rendered desperate, as it was thought that they believed that the British could close upon them at any time and kill them. They drank *chang* (a native intoxicant), which made them frantic, and they rushed up to our breastworks, only to be shot down in scores. On the 2nd August they lost over 200 killed and 400 wounded, while 9 men on our side were killed and 36 wounded.

An officer graphically describes the British camp during this anxious time in the following manner:—

What a sight our camp would be, even to those who visited Sebastopol! The long lines of tents, the thatched hovels of the native servants, the rows of horses, the parks of artillery, the British soldier in his grey linen coat and trousers, the dark Sikhs with their red and blue turbans, the Afghans with the same, their wild air and coloured saddlecloths, and the little Ghoorkas dressed up like demons of ugliness in black worsted Kilmarnock bonnets and woollen coats. The soldiers are loitering through the lines or in the bazaars. Suddenly an alarm is sounded, and everyone rushes to his tent. The infantry soldier seizes his musket and slings on his pouch; the artilleryman gets his guns horsed; the Afghan rides out to explore, and in a few minutes, everyone is in his place.

The enemy were very desperate on the first day of August—the festival of the Eed, or the anniversary of the sacrifice which Abraham meant to make of Isaac, and they made an attempt to get their guns across the canal, but the temporary bridge which they had erected was carried away by a flood, and they had to retire. It was an awful night, that of the 2nd of August, with the roar of the guns, the rattle of musketry, the yells of the savage rebels, and the cheers of our men. When the morning broke, 22 of our men were found to be killed, while over 200 rebels lay dead in front of our breastworks. The religious frenzy passed off, and the rebels settled down more quietly in the city, while Brigadier Wilson waited for reinforcements, which were by this time hurrying up for the all-important capture of Delhi.

CHAPTER 18

The Battles at Delhi (continued): 1857

Brigadier Wilson was badly in want of help, and there was joy in the camp when Brigadier Nicholson marched in one day towards the middle of August at the head of 1,000 Europeans and 1,400 Sikhs, while he was also able to report the advance of a siege train from Ferozepore.

There was now a more formidable force concentrated before Delhi, which might be set down at about 10,000 fighting men, of whom nearly 5,000 were Europeans.

Not long after Nicholson's arrival, information was received in the British camp that the enemy contemplated a move whereby they might cut off the supplies. The exact nature of the tidings was that about 7,000 rebels had marched out of Delhi, with a view to crossing the Nujuffghur Jheel Drain, and that the army was supported by 18 guns. Brigadier Nicholson organised a movable column, and marched on the morning of the 25th August to turn the enemy. His force consisted of a squadron of lancers, the Guide cavalry, H.M. 61st Foot, 1st European Fusiliers, Cokes Rifles, 2nd Punjaub Infantry, Major Tombs' Horse Artillery, and Remington's troops, with, the Mooltan Horse.

A party of sappers were also included in the column, to blow up the bridge at Nujuffghur, making in all a force of 1,000 European and 2,000 native troops. The column marched for about ten miles, when the brigadier learned that the enemy had crossed the bridge and were preparing to encamp at Nujuffghur. He pushed on with all speed, and, after another long march, came up to the village, from which he was assailed by a vigorous fire of cannon and musketry, which was directed against the head of the column.

The general ordered his men forward, and told them to reserve their fire until the last possible minute. The flank of the attacking line were supported by the artillery, and these went forward at a gallop, concentrating their fire upon a *serai* which the enemy were defending with four guns. Sharply and clearly came the order from the gallant Nicholson—"The line will advance," and as if on parade the soldiers, with bayonets on the slant, rushed forward, and with a rousing cheer they rushed upon the enemy, who flinched at the appearance of the bayonet. The four captured guns were turned upon the flying rebels, who took up a position at the bridge. Here they attempted to make a show of resistance, but the stand was a brief one. Their lines were soon broken by our relentless artillery fire, and four more guns fell into our hands.

The rebels managed to carry off three guns, and when our troops went forward to hold it while the sappers prepared a mine underneath for its destruction, they opened a heavy fire upon our lines. In the midst of the fire the advanced company held the bridge until the sappers had done their work. The mine was sprung, the arch disappeared, and the troops retired to take a well-earned rest Brigadier Nicholson had completely baffled the enemy and captured thirteen guns, besides killing and wounding hundreds of the rebels. The British loss amounted to about 120 slain, yet it was a cheerful company that returned to camp, for the soldiers knew that they had done their duty.

A few days later there was a murmur in the air, for through the British lines flew the intelligence that General Wilson had at last determined upon a grand assault on the city. A general order was promulgated by the general, from which we make the following quotation, to show the spirit in which our soldiers went forward in the work of vengeance:—

The artillery will have even harder work than they have had, and which they have so well and cheerfully performed hitherto; this, however, will be for a short period only; and, when ordered to the assault, the major-general feels assured that British pluck and determination will carry everything before them, and that the bloodthirsty and murderous mutineers against whom they are fighting will be driven headlong out of their stronghold and exterminated. But to enable them to do this, he warns the troops of the absolute necessity of their keeping together and not straggling from their columns. By this only can success be assured.

Major-General Wilson need hardly remind the troops of the cruel murders committed on their officers and comrades, their wives and children, to move them in the deadly struggle. No quarter should be given to the mutineers! At the same time, for the sake of humanity, and the honour of the country they belong to, he calls upon them to spare all women and children that may come in their way.

There was an unusual stir in the camp, for the soldiers moved about with a business-like air which showed their pleasure at being at last permitted to rush like an avalanche upon the city. The cautious Wilson did nothing rash, but saw that every part of his fighting machine was in thorough order. The soldiers were now fresh and ready, while the promised siege train put in an appearance. It came in on the morning of 4th September, consisting of forty heavy guns, mortars and howitzers, with vast supplies of ammunition. It was well supported by a wing of the 8th or King's Regiment, two companies of the 61st, and a wing of the Belooch battalion. Two days later arrived a squadron of the 9th Lancers, artillery recruits from Meerut, and 200 of the 60th Rifles, while the 4th Punjaub Infantry, the Jheend Rajah's levies, and the Cashmere Dograhs arrived two days later.

The force was especially strong in artillery, for the reason that the walls and gates had to be battered down before breaches for the assault by the infantry could be attempted. The rebels in the town were singularly quiet, but they could not miss seeing the great preparations that were going on in the British camp. They were not now the smart troops that had been drilled by British officers in the days before they had been incited to rebellion. They were fanatical, and therefore unreliable, and although they could be trusted to make a good fight for their lives, they were an undisciplined and riotous crew.

If that could be said of the *sepoys*, words fail to describe the character of the mercenaries who clung to the fringe of the rebel army. They were the scum of the country, arrant cowards who gloried in the butchery of defenceless women and children. The batteries were well mounted, and everything was prepared in a manner for the warm reception of the *Feringhees*. Every *sepoy* and rebel knew that it meant certain death to fall into the hands of the British, so, making the best of their position, they resolved to fight for their lives.

The bombardment of Delhi proper opened on the 11th of September, when nine 24-pounders opened on the towers and walls at the Cashmere gate. Other guns directed their fire upon the same position, and a ceaseless fire was kept up, so that two days later it was seen that two breaches had been made practicable for escalade near the Cashmere and Water Bastions. On the 14th September, the whole force moved out of camp in three columns to the assault. Major Reid, in charge of the column which consisted of Ghoorkas and Cashmere levies, attacked the Kishengunze and Pahareepore suburbs, but were driven back with heavy loss. The rebels defended desperately, and made big gaps in the British lines.

Brigadier Nicholson was at the head of another column, and he stormed the Cashmere bastion, driving the rebels like chaff before him. His men could not stop, and reached the Lahore gate, where Nicholson, their brave leader, fell mortally wounded. Brigadier Jones had meantime scaled the breach at the Water bastion, and aided Colonel Campbell in bursting open the gate. The assault had thus practically been attended with complete success at all parts, and although the loss was severe, yet the hardest part of the work had been performed.

It was necessary that the Cashmere gate should be blown up, and this was one of the most daring exploits of the attack. The party in charge of the explosives was commanded by Lieutenants Horne and Salkeld, and consisted of Sergeants Smith, Carmichael, and Corporal Burgess of the Royal Sappers and Miners, Bugler Hawthorne of the 52nd Foot, and 24 native sappers, who were covered by the fire of the 60th Rifles. The whole force rushed towards the gate, bearing the powder, under a heavy fire from the enemy.

The drawbridge over the ditch had been destroyed, but the brave men crossed over on planks, and soon had the powder-bags against the gate, with the enemy firing at them through a wicket. Sergeant Carmichael was killed while laying the powder, and while Lieutenant Salkeld was preparing to light the charge, he was shot through an arm and leg. He was in time to hand the match to Corporal Burgess who had no sooner fired the train than he fell, mortally wounded.

The survivors of the gallant little party took shelter, and in a few moments the huge Cashmere gate was blown to atoms. Lieutenant Horne at once ordered the bugler to sound the advance to his regiment—the 52nd—and so great was the din that he had to sound three times before the order was understood. Bravely the Oxford Light Infantry, with fixed bayonets, under Colonel Campbell, advanced and secured the barrier, driving the rebels before them in wild confusion.

The city had now been entered, and the British troops, still keeping in formation of columns, marched through the stately streets, which had been the scenes of such terrible brutalities. The British soldiers shot and bayonetted every rebel that came in their path, and drove the cowed *sepoys* before them like dumb driven cattle.

As evening came on, the British attack was allowed to slacken, but it had been a brave day's work. The whole line of works from the Water bastion to the Cabul gate, including the Cashmere and Moree gates and bastions, were in our hands, and also the church, college, and a number of private houses. Altogether we held the northern part of Delhi, and, considering the impregnable nature of the defences, and the sheer desperation which the natives threw into their fighting, this immense advantage had been gained at a comparatively slight cost.

The enemy, who had suffered severely, fled from the vicinity of the captured position, but they had not yet evacuated the city, and the next day was employed by the British in strengthening their position and directing a heavy fire upon the magazine. The *sepoys* never came into actual hand to hand conflict with our men, for their marked repugnance to the bayonet deterred them, but they continued to skirmish and snipe at the British troops. The well-directed fire upon the magazine had good effect, for before evening a breach had been made.

This was all that was required, and although the mutineers flocked to this point to defend the gap, the 61st gallantly rushed to storm it. There were a few straggling volleys from the enemy, but only one or two guns on the bastions belched forth. Calmly, as if on parade, the 61st went on—a line of scarlet tipped with steel. They had the dreaded bayonet fixed, and as they neared the gap which had been made in the wall, they broke into the double, and literally hurled themselves at the breach. The craven-hearted rebels were awed by such a charge, they recklessly fired a volley which did no damage, and, with a last look at the oncoming avengers, turned and fled.

The gunners on the walls were seized with a similar terror, and they dropped their lighted port-fires and fled without discharging any of the six guns, heavily charged with grape, which commanded the breach. Through the night of the 16th, when the assault by the 61st was made, the British troops wrought great havoc amongst the mutineers. The bayonets were busy, and our sharpshooters had excellent practice in bringing down any rebel who had the courage to show his swarthy face above cover.

Next day the bank, which had been the scene of bloodshed when the mutineers invested the city, fell into our hands, along with the extensive grounds in the midst of which it is situated. General Wilson became cognisant of its importance as a position, and when he moved his guns into the grounds, the Royal Palace, from which the king and the princes had made their escape, was as good as doomed.

The palace, as already indicated, is more of a fortress than a place of residence, and with capable defenders, might have defied an investing army for some time. It was imperative that it should be taken, so our guns battered the stoutly-built walls, while shells were directed over the complete line of buildings.

The resistance was feeble, and when once an entrance had been obtained, the rebels and royal bodyguard fled in all directions, seemingly not desirous of encountering the British troops. The palace was soon completely in our hands, and large numbers of rebels who sought to defend their abdicated master were at once cut down, while those who were fortunate enough to escape through the grounds, either fell into the hands of our men posted at various quarters, or were killed by the avenging troops which dashed along the streets of Delhi.

The order of the general to have no mercy upon the rebels was carried up to the letter, and although many of the wretches begged and prayed for their lives, it is to their credit as a brave race that it must be said that they met their death bravely in the majority of cases. The women and children were respected, and sent to places of safety.

A story is related of a veteran of the 60th Regiment, who, along with a small detachment, was engaged ferreting out the rebels. They had come across a band of *sepoys*, women, and children mixed into a heterogeneous mass, and, covering the group with their rifles, called on the men to step aside. This they sullenly did, while the women, who were apparently their wives, stood at a distance, quite well aware of what was to happen. Although ordered to depart, they preferred to stay and see their mutinous partners perish. One of the women clung to the knees of the veteran soldier, who was about to administer the *coup de grace* to a sinister looking rebel. "Oh, *Sahib*, he is my husband!"

"Weel, ma guid wumman," grimly responded the son of Mars, "ye're going to be a weedy sune!" and with that he drove his bayonet through the rebel's heart. "Noo, mistress," he continued, as he surveyed his reeking blade, "if ye ha'e ony mair freends like yer departed husband, jist tak' me tae them, an' I'll be pleased to gie them the same medicine!"

This aptly illustrates the callousness of our soldiers' hearts. They could forgive foes who had killed in fair battle, but they could not bring themselves to spare fiends who had killed and outraged their fair countrywomen.

With the falling of the palace into our hands, the greatest stronghold of the rebels had gone from their grasp. The Jumna Musjid, a palatial building which the mutineers had converted into a fortress, also fell after a heavy attack, in which a number of lives were lost.

In these operations no fewer than 205 pieces of cannon were captured, while a vast quantity of munitions of war fell into our hands. It must not be supposed that all these advantages were gained without heavy loss to our troops. The storming of the gates and breaches was the most dangerous work, and it was at these attacks that the greatest number of lives were lost. There were 8 European officers and 162 rank and file killed, with 103 natives, while 52 officers, 510 rank and file, and 310 natives were wounded. It is impossible to gauge the rebel loss, but it is computed that at the grand assault on the city over 5,000 perished, and this death-roll was added to day after day by our pursuing soldiers.

The king, along with his two sons, had fled from Delhi by a secret exit, when the British gained admission to the city. He fled to the tomb of Hoomayon, situated just outside the city. This fine building, which is surmounted by a gigantic dome, served as their hiding-place for a short period, but eventually Captain Hodson of the Guides discovered their retreat, and as it was necessary that they should be captured, he proceeded with his force to the place where they were concealed.

He called upon the occupants to surrender, and although they were inclined to treat for terms, the captain was inflexible, and demanded unconditional surrender. The king, who had attained the patriarchal age of ninety years, had really played an unimportant part in the insurrection, and had merely been set up as a royal figurehead by the mutineers. The captain, having respect for his grey hairs, spared his life, and also that of the Begum Zeenah Mahal.

The sons of the king had, no doubt much against their will, been actively engaged in the mutiny, and although they were but milk-and-water soldiers, they had chosen to act as leaders, and deserved death. A native of Delhi, writing regarding these persons says:—

The princes are made officers in the royal army; thousands of pities for the poor luxurious princes! They are sometimes compelled to go out of the gates of the city in the heat of the sun; their hearts palpitate from the firing of muskets and guns. Unfortunately, they do not know how to command an army, and their forces laugh at their imperfections and bad arrangements.

Captain Hodson gave orders that the two princes and a grandson of the king should be shot, and this was done in the city, their naked bodies being hung by the neck in the *Kotwallee*, or Mayor's Court, in presence of the people, who were awed at the fate of those who had ruled them. Executions were common in the city, which was now wholly in possession of the queen's troops.

General Wilson had earned through his trying part with honour, and completed his task when, in the palace of the Great Mogul he drained a goblet with his other officers to the health of Her Majesty, as Empress of India, while the soldiers cheered, and sang "God Save the Queen."

With the capture of Delhi and all its attendant excitement there ensued a time of peace for the troops at Delhi, but they were fated to lose the services of the dauntless Wilson. The general's health, which had never been of a robust nature, completely broke down, and he had reluctantly to resign his command, being succeeded at Delhi by Brigadier-General Penny, C.B

Delhi had been the great focus of the rebellion, the gathering place of the rebels, and now that they had met with ignominious defeat, those who escaped from the avenging army made their way to the surrounding towns, inciting those whom they met to rise against the British.

The rebels had tasted defeat, but they trusted to their overwhelming numbers to bring them victory. While they held Delhi, they had inspired the mutineers in other districts by their success, and now that they had lost this important point they as rapidly as possible transferred their operations to the surrounding provinces, where weaker forces met their attack.

Agra and Lucknow became their headquarters, and they fully anticipated wiping out the small garrisons quartered there. In Delhi, the citizens who had been driven to serve the mutineers during their tenure, were only too glad to throw in their lot with the British, and the work of repair and reclamation went steadily on. The troops were seldom idle in pursuing the enemy, and Colonel Greathed of the 84th went after them at the head of a large force. At the military cantonment at Secunderabad there was found a vast quantity of plundered property which had been stolen from the poor unfortunates who perished in Delhi, and the sight of the women's dresses, hats, and bonnets so exasperated the 84th, that they set fire to the whole place.

At Bolundshuhur the enemy made a show of resistance with light guns at the junction of two crossroads. Our heavy cannon soon silenced the rebels' pieces, and the cavalry dashing into the town drove the cringing and affrighted rebels before them. Still keeping up the work of clearing the district, the Fort of Malaghur, which consisted of eight bastions, was blown up. It was while executing this work that brave Lieutenant Horne, who, it will be remembered, led the sappers at the explosion of the Cashmere gate, was accidentally killed by the premature explosion of one of his own mines.

It was now evident that the mutineers were endeavouring to concentrate their scattered forces at Agra, an important and well-fortified British position. Brigadier Greathed judiciously sent his wounded to Meerut, and started on the heels of the mutineers, coming up with them at Alighur, in the *doab* of the Ganges, and a little over 50 miles from Agra. The rebels made every show of giving our troops trouble, but when once their guns had been silenced, they lost heart, for they could not stand to meet the shock of a bayonet charge; and few can blame them when it is remembered that the finest troops in the world had reeled and broken against the onslaught of the glittering steel propelled by the brawny arms of a rough Highlander. The mutineers were continually losing men since their flight from Delhi, and in this engagement, they must have lost fully 400 in killed alone.

On the 10th of October, 1857, without seeing any other bands of fleeing rebels, the brigadier entered Agra, the key to Western India. They imagined themselves safe from molestation, and proceeded to pitch camp. While they were doing so a battery of guns belched out a heavy fire upon the troops, and a body of cavalry galloped amongst the men, inflicting heavy loss.

Never was surprise more complete, but our soldiers soon recovered, and before the enemy could fire a sixth round, our guns were replying, while our troops were drawn up in position. The ambushed and cunning foe was soon unearthed, and, afraid to give open battle, they fled. The troops dashed after them, and over a thousand rebels were killed, 14 guns taken, along with a vast quantity of stores and plunder.

The rebels were now split and scattered, and this force of Mhow rebels who had been unaware of the arrival of Greathed's large force, were practically disbanded for the time being. Sir James Hope Grant in another direction caught up with the Delhi fugitives at the ancient city of Canonj, and killed hundreds without mercy.

It will thus be evident that the murders of Delhi were well avenged, and Delhi and its surrounding country swept perfectly clear of rebels. Delhi had been dearly won, but it was the turning point in the mutiny, and the mutineers had received a check and a lesson which told upon their subsequent fighting.

Chapter 19

The Battles at Cawnpore: 1857

Cawnpore stands out written in letters of blood in the annals of British history, and ranks as one of the bloodiest episodes of the terrible mutiny in our Indian Empire in 1857. It is chiefly conspicuous for the inhuman massacre of innocent men and women and the butchery of little children by the orders of Nana Sahib, that fiend in human form, who was destined to become the central figure of the mutiny.

He first came into prominence at the investment of Cawnpore, and his blood thirst mess chilled the hearts of the brave defenders, yet roused deep feelings of revenge in those who came to the relief. General Wheeler was in command at Cawnpore—a brave and tried officer, who would fight to the last: and, being distrustful of a regiment of Oude Irregulars, disbanded them and sent for a single company of the 32nd from Lucknow.

All was quietness at this time—the 3rd of June—at Cawnpore, when news reached Wheeler that the garrison at Lucknow were in sore straits. He immediately sent back the company of the 32nd, and, as an additional reinforcement, ordered a detachment of the 84th to accompany them. This had the effect of thinning the Cawnpore garrison, which now consisted of 60 men of the 84th regiment, 70 of the 32nd, and 15 of the Madras Fusiliers, with a few artillerymen and six guns. Two native regiments were still within the lines—the 1st and 56th Native Infantry; but as a precaution, the general ordered that they should sleep outside the lines.

The dreaded outbreak came at last, and the first shot was fired on the morning of the 6th of June. Immediately the defenders rushed to the entrenchments to repel an expected attack of the rebel cavalry and infantry, but the first day's fighting was mostly confined to an artillery duel.

The enemy were vastly superior as regards big guns, and their shots proved very destructive to the walls of the barracks. Wheeler's only hope was to last out until relief came, but gradually the enemy closed in, capturing the compounds, bungalows, and other buildings, from which they poured in a perfect hail of bullets upon the brave defenders. Captain John Moore, of the 32nd, did yeoman service in checking these encroachments, and, although wounded in the arm, he sallied out on two occasions at the head of 25 men and spiked the nearest guns.

The deadly fire of the rebels was not the only danger, for the heat was so intense that the death-rate among the women and children became alarming. As soon as they died, their bodies were laid out on the verandah to await the coming of night, when they were cast into a well.

The rebels, desperate to achieve their end, commenced to fire hot shells and red-hot shot, which caused a part of the barracks to ignite. Unfortunately, this was the very part where the sick and wounded were lying. Before anything could be done, about forty poor creatures had perished in the flames, while the defenders could not quit their posits in the trenches lest the savage horde would burst in and annihilate the garrison. The barracks soon became so riddled that they afforded but little protection, and the women had to burrow in the earth to find safety for themselves and their children.

Theirs was a terrible plight, with shells screaming over them, and the foul stench of decaying horses and cattle for ever in their nostrils. It should be mentioned that the survivors of the garrison at Futtehghur, which had been abandoned, to the number of 126, men, women and children, had taken refuge in Cawnpore, where they were lodged in the assembly rooms. They had escaped in boats down the Ganges, and many lives had been lost through the rebels firing upon them from the banks. Little did they dream that a more terrible fate awaited them.

On the eighteenth day of the siege, Nana Sahib sent an old English lady, named Mrs. Greenway, whom he had captured, to the barracks, to offer honourable terms of surrender to General Wheeler. These were to the effect that all government money should be given up, that the force should march out under arms with 60 rounds of ammunition to every man, and that boats, properly victualled, should be in readiness at the landing-stage on the Ganges, about a mile from the British entrenchment.

These terms were signed, sealed, and ratified on the solemn oath of the *Nana*. Hostilities at once ceased, and General Wheeler made

THE BATTLE OF CAWNPORE.—RECOVERING THE GUNS.

preparations to evacuate the place which he had so gallantly defended against fearful odds. On the 27th of June, the force, to the number of about 700, marched down to the boats, little thinking of the treachery that was working in the heart of the *Nana*. There were nearly 300 women and children there, and they took their places in the boats.

The moment all were embarked, *Nana*, gave the signal, and a fierce musketry fire rained upon the trusting and hapless band in the frail boats. Then ensued a terrible massacre, hundreds being killed without a chance of defending themselves, while those who sought safety in the water were shot as soon as they showed themselves. Those in the boat which contained the gallant Wheeler and his daughter made a gallant resistance, and actually succeeded in getting downstream, only to be captured by three of the *Nana's* boats and brought back to Cawnpore.

The men were separated from the women, and the *Nana* ordered them to be shot by men of the 1st Bengal Infantry.

"No! no!" answered several of the rebels. "We will not shoot Wheeler Sahib, for he made the name of our regiment great."

There were others who were ready enough to perpetrate the foul deed. The women threw themselves upon the breasts of those whom they loved, and begged to share their fate. They were rudely dragged apart, and just as the rebels were about to fire, the chaplain asked to be allowed to read prayers before they died. This was granted, and after he had read a few prayers, the doomed men clasped hands in a last lingering goodbye. Crack went the rifles, and in a minute, they were all shot down, while those who were wounded were soon despatched. So ended the first chapter of the *Nana's* treachery.

The women and children, to the number of 122, were taken to the *Nana's* house, and a few days later, along with the fugitives from Futtehghur, were removed to the assembly rooms.

Such fiendish brutality could not go unpunished, and when tidings of the massacre reached Britain, Brigadier-General Havelock was ordered to place himself at the head of a force to march on Cawnpore and Lucknow.

It was not a very pretentious army that left Allahabad on the 7th of July—some 1,300 Europeans; but the presence of 600 men of the 78th Highlanders in the ranks gave it additional strength. Major Renaud had been sent on with a small force as advance guard, and Havelock coming up with him, the united forces encamped at Khaga, about five miles from Futtehghur. While the camp was being pitched,

MASSACRE IN THE BOATS OFF CAWNPORE

the enemy, numbering 3,500 with 12 guns, was observed, and orders were given for an immediate action. Captain Maude pushed on his guns to point blank range, and terrorised the enemy with his fire. Against a combined British advance, the rebels retreated, leaving their guns behind them.

It was almost a bloodless victory, for the British loss was trifling, while the advantage gained was of immense importance. Worn out with a long march, Havelock decided to rest, and this gave the rebels time to take up another defensive position to block the road to Cawnpore.

Havelock resumed his march on the 14th, and came up with the enemy at Aong. The resistance made was but feeble, and under a galling fire of round and grape shot they once more retreated to the bridge over the Pandoo Nuddee, which was the last obstacle on the road to Cawnpore. What the withering artillery fire failed to do, the bayonets of the Highlanders accomplished, and, leaving a number of guns and ammunition behind, the rebels were soon in full retreat to join the *Nana's* main force at Cawnpore.

When the *Nana* learned of the defeat of his troops, he determined upon the slaughter of every European in Cawnpore. About four o'clock on the afternoon of the 15th, the bloody butchery began. The males were ordered out and immediately shot, but the women refused to move, and neither threats or persuasions would induce them.

They clung to each other until at last the enraged *sepoys* discharged muskets from the windows amongst the poor unfortunates. They then rushed in with sword and bayonet, and soon the place was a reeking shambles. Fiercely the maddened brutes slashed and stabbed amongst the quivering mass. They heeded not the pitiful prayers for mercy, but killed women and children alike. There were about 150 women and children in the room, and soon the floor was piled high with bleeding bodies. The massacre continued for several hours, and at last, thinking that their work was complete, the murderers of the pure and innocent desisted.

Next morning it was found that a number had escaped death by hiding under heaps of bodies, and orders were given to recommence the butchery. Terrified and mad with suffering, the poor creatures, drenched with the blood of their countrywomen, seized their children, and, rushing over the compound, cast themselves into a well, preferring such a death to excruciating torture at the hands of the *Nana's* myrmidons. That same evening the other mangled bodies were

CAWNPORE, 1857

cast into the well, and the *Nana's* bloody work was completed.

Since that dreadful day a mausoleum has been erected over the well—"Sacred to the perpetual memory of a great company of Christian people, chiefly women and children, xvi. day of July, MDCCCL-VII," and guarded by the sublime figure of an angel standing at the cross, to keep watch and ward for aye o'er Britain's noble dead.

Meanwhile, Havelock's troops, unaware of the foul deed which had been enacted within the walls of the city, moved rapidly on, and on the 16th halted at the village of Maharajpoor, before engaging the *Nana*, who was posted in a strong position about two miles off at the village of Aherwa. He had cut up and rendered impassable both roads, and his heavy guns, seven in number, were disposed along his position, which consisted of a series of villages. Behind were the infantry, composed of the mutineers and his own armed followers, numbering in all about 5,000.

General Havelock quickly grasped the situation, and decided upon a flanking movement. The column, therefore, after a short, frontal advance, veered off to the right, and circled round the enemy's left. The *Nana*, observing this move, sent a large body of horse to the left, and at once opened fire upon the British column with all his guns. Still Havelock achieved his object, and turned the enemy's left Forming into line, the British guns were soon playing upon the batteries, while the infantry, covered by a wing of the Madras Fusiliers as skirmishers, advanced in direct echelon of regiments from the right.

Then came the moment for the Highlanders, as three guns of the enemy were strongly posted behind a lofty eminence, and these had to be taken. Under Colonel Hamilton, the 78th moved forward under a steady fire. They reached the guns and charged with fixed bayonets, but the enemy broke and fled. Meanwhile the 64th and 84th regiments had not been idle, engaging the enemy hotly on the left, and capturing two guns. General Havelock now re-formed his force on account of the retreat of Nana Sahib to a new position to the rear of his first and nearer Cawnpore. The British infantry changed line to the front and rear while the guns were brought up.

While this was being done, the *Nana*, despatching his cavalry to the rear of the British force, attacked from this point. They charged fiercely, but the British, volleys were too much for them, and they withdrew. In the van the fighting was stubborn, and the rebel infantry seemed to be in disorderly retreat when a reserve 24-pounder came to the rescue, and played considerable havoc amongst the British lines. The infantry once more rallied, and the cavalry rejoined the *Nana's* forces.

It was imperative that the 24-pounder should be silenced, as the Madras Fusiliers, the 64th, 78th, and 84th, formed in line, were losing heavily. The rebel skirmishers were becoming bolder and, getting within range, poured a heavy musketry fire upon the stolid British ranks. To make matters worse, the tired oxen could not bring up the guns over the rough road.

The general gave orders for another steady advance. It seemed madness to go forward amid such a storm of shot and shell, but Havelock knew his men.

No firing, 64th and 78th. Trust to the bayonet, and remember that I am with you.

These words inspired the men with a fresh courage, so, with a ringing cheer, they dashed forward. Steadily they advanced, the enemy sending round shot into the ranks up to 300 yards' range, and then poured a perfect fusillade of grape. The 64th were directly in line of the gun, and suffered severely, but when the order to "Charge!" came, each man bounded forward.

The rebels did not wait for the bayonet, but broke and fled, with the British in pursuit, showing no mercy to the fugitives. The *Nana's* forces were now in total confusion, and retired upon Cawnpore. The British guns were now up, and a heavy fire was opened upon the retreating host. The battle was over, and the tired troops halted for the night, while the wounded were attended and the dead interred. The British loss was found to be about 100 killed and wounded, which does not say much for the rebel fire, seeing that they had practically target shooting for a considerable time. The enemy's loss was severe, as the dead and dying strewed the road to Cawnpore.

Hardly had the troops settled down to rest when a tremendous explosion shook the earth. Nana Sahib, recognising his defeat, had blown up the Cawnpore magazine, and abandoned the place, with which his name will be for ever darkly associated.

Next day Havelock's force entered Cawnpore, to find that they were too late; a glance at the blood-bespattered room and the ghastly sight of the mangled bodies in the well spoke all too plainly of the fearful carnage. It was to find this that the brave force had marched 126 miles, defeated the enemy four times, and captured 24 guns. Little wonder that the brave soldiers were maddened by such a spectacle; little wonder that they swore terrible oaths of vengeance.

One of the officers of the 78th wrote:—

I wept when I looked into the room where the massacre had
taken place, and saw the blood on the floor and walls, portions
of clothing, and shreds of hair which had been torn from the
innocent heads of our women and children. And I was not the
only one to weep, for I saw old and hardened soldiers, who had
endured the carnage of many a battlefield without a tremor,
with tears running down their tanned cheeks.

No mercy was shown to the rebels who were caught. First of all,
they were compelled to clean up a portion of the bloodstained floor,
and as to touch blood is abhorrent to the high-caste natives (they
thinking that by doing so they are doomed to perdition), this was
a terrible punishment. They were then hanged, and Brigadier Neill,
who had now command at Cawnpore, was successful in sending many
to their just doom.

Large numbers of the enemy still hung about in the vicinity of
Cawnpore, and the troops made several successful sorties. The *Nana*
had wisely quitted the field, and had taken refuge in his palace at
Bithoor, where he was strongly supported. The skirmishing bands of
mutineers which molested the Cawnpore garrison were gradually
driven back, and must have suffered severely. An incident, gruesome
it may be, is related of a stalwart Highlander, who had taken part in
one of the skirmishes. He was discovered standing musing and gazing
intently upon two headless corpses which lay upon the ground.

"What's troubling you, my man?" said an officer who chanced to
be near.

"Lo'd, sir, I sliced aff baith their heads, and noo I dinna ken the ane
fae the ither, so I doot I'll need toe lat them lie as they are"; and, as if
playine football, he kicked the heads aside.

There were others who put notches on their guns a notch for
every rebel they killed.

Knowing what their fate would be if they were taken prisoner,
the mutineers gradually fell back to join the *Nana's* main force. It was
Havelock's intention to march immediately to the relief of Lucknow,
but his force was sadly in need of rest. At last, all was in readiness, and
on the 25th of July he set out at the head of his small band of 1,500
men to give battle to countless thousands. Henceforward the stirring
scenes of the mutiny were transferred to other fields than Cawnpore.

But Cawnpore was destined to undergo another siege, as the

Gwalior contingent of rebels, an inactive plundering and bloodthirsty band, had determined to strike a blow at the city which had been the scene of such terrible massacres. Havelock had relieved Lucknow at this time, and Sir Colin Campbell had gone to the rescue of the force that had to remain shut up there. Fortunately, they delayed their projected attack until Campbell had forced an entrance to Lucknow, but when they appeared in large numbers before Cawnpore, on the 26th of November, the position of the weakened garrison in the city was a perilous one.

The rebels drew up at the Pandoo Nuddee, a few miles from Cawnpore. The forts which had previously been used in repelling the *Nana's* attacks were strengthened, and General Wyndham, who had won glory at the Redan in the Crimea, felt confident of holding the mutineers at bay until Sir Colin Campbell returned with Havelock from Lucknow. When the enemy were sighted at the Pandoo Nuddee, he determined to show them that he did not require to act upon the defensive, but that, if occasion presented itself, he could also attack.

He determined to have the first blow, but it is feared that the bold and intrepid general vastly underestimated the enemy's strength. He marched out to check the rebels at the head of about 2,000 men, composed of the 64th, 82nd, and 88th regiments, along with a section of the 34th. He came up with the enemy, and at once opened fire, which was smartly returned by the insurgents from guns which were judiciously posted, and which commanded the British position.

Wyndham saw that he had a superior force arrayed against him, but, trusting to the valour of his men, he renewed the attack. Against the odds the sterling prowess of the British soldier had good effect, and the enemy, menaced with the bayonet, fell back in the direction of their guns, leaving a number of killed and wounded on the field. The pursuit was kept up for a short distance, and resistance was offered by the rebel cavalry, who repeatedly charged to protect their retreating infantry.

These half-hearted charges were easily repulsed by steady volleying from our ranks, which emptied several saddles. The cavalry, however, undoubtedly saved the infantry, which stood in danger of being cut up by Wyndham's infuriated troops.

The gallantry of the little band of the 34th deserves high commendation. They threw themselves into squares to deal with the cavalry, and did terrible execution in the ranks. It was during the fight with the cavalry that Captain Day of the 88th. who had fought in all the battles of the Crimea, struck by a musket ball and fell into a well, from which his body was never recovered.

While the shades of evening were falling over the bloodstained field, General Wyndham ordered the troops to fall back. This they were nothing loth to do, as they had had a hard day's fighting, and were glad to encamp for the night on the Jewee plain. The camp was well situated, having a thick covering of trees and brushwood in the direction of the enemy, a brick kiln on one side, with the city in the rear to fall back upon if occasion should arise. Meanwhile the rebels had not been idle, and having made sure that the British had given up the pursuit, they also halted and commenced to beat up reinforcements.

In the early morning they advanced upon the British position to the number of 14,000 infantry and cavalry, with no fewer than 40 guns. General Wyndham, no doubt imagining that if the worst came to the worst he had the city to fall back upon, stuck to his guns when the enemy's fire began. There was a perfect hail of shot amongst the brushwood, and the rebel gunners had so accurate a range as 'to throw the British troops into confusion at certain parts. Officers gave orders and then contradicted them, the result being that Wyndham had no plan of attack or defence. Men were falling rapidly, and the rebel infantry, under the cover of their big guns, prepared to advance. There was nothing for it but to retire, and so hurried was the retreat that the tents and baggage had to be left behind while the troops took refuge behind the entrenchments.

This success made the rebels bolder, so that on the 28th, after forming a junction with Nana Sahib's troops, they prepared to attack the entrenchments. They quickly captured the bungalows, and partially demolished houses in the vicinity, and practically succeeded in surrounding the British position on every side save that which fronted the river. This advantage was not gained without severe loss, for the fire of the British was most effective. Still, it was an immense advantage, and for a time it appeared as if the whole force would be annihilated. The mutineers opened fire from their left and r-entre with light and heavy guns, driving in our outposts to within a short distance of our own guns.

Inch by inch the ground was stubbornly contested, and certainly there was no lack of courage displayed by the defenders. The assembly rooms, with all their contents, consisting of 11,000 rounds of ball cartridge, the mess plate of four Queen's regiments, along with the trophies of the 34th, and an immense quantity of private property, fell into the hands of the rebels. Elated with success, and gloating over the prospect of a second massacre, they attacked with greater vigour than had ever been displayed in previous engagements. There were many brave deeds that day, and one deserves special notice.

A party of the 64th regiment, only thirty strong, under Captain Wright, held the Baptist Chapel and old burial ground. Finding he was being surrounded, he opened out, and, skirmishing, kept the *sepoys* at bay. The gallant captain noticed a wing of the 64th marching out, 250 strong, to capture four guns which had done great damage to the British left. Captain Wright dashed forward to act as advance guard to his comrades, and the 64th, without pausing to count the cost, plunged in and spiked three before the gunners had recovered from their surprise.

Although vastly outnumbered, the 64th did great execution with the bayonet, and this was the first real check the enemy had received that day. Unfortunately, Captain Mackinnon and Lieutenant Gordon were captured by the rebels, and, although wounded, were murdered in cold blood

The sailors and rifles came up and captured three 18-pounders and two mortars. This check on the enemy proved the salvation of Cawnpore, for it compelled the enemy to slacken fire. The defenders settled down to a night's fighting, but ere the daylight died, resounding cheers rang through Cawnpore, for deliverance had come, in the shape of Sir Colin Campbell, who had heard the roar of the guns and had pushed on with all speed. The old campaigner took in the situation at a glance, and, assuming command, he at once saw to the safety of his own troops, who rested during the night.

Next morning the rebels opened a cross fire from flanks and centre, which was replied to from our guns in the entrenchments. The sick and wounded from Lucknow, along with the women and children, were safely sheltered, but next, day the rebel cannon playing upon the hospital did some damage. Sir Colin was plainly biding his time, and meanwhile, he had sent the invalids and women and children to Allahabad. The 93rd Highlanders did noble service in spiking the gun and repelling assaults. On the morning of 6th December every battery and gun was trained upon the enemy's positions in the town, and all day long a storm of shot and shell raged over the town.

Next day saw the rebels evacuate the town, but if they bargained to escape, they were wrong, for Sir Colin drove home the blow, and such regiments as the Black Watch and the 93rd did fearful execution amongst the flying cowards along the Calpee road. Sir James Hope Grant pursued them further, and administered the *coup de grace*, for the Gwalior contingent was nevermore heard of, and, thanks to Sir Colin Campbell, Cawnpore was once more saved.

LEONAUR

ALSO FROM LEONAUR
AVAILABLE IN SOFTCOVER OR HARDCOVER WITH DUST JACKET

THE FALL OF THE MOGHUL EMPIRE OF HINDUSTAN *by H. G. Keene*—By the beginning of the nineteenth century, as British and Indian armies under Lake and Wellesley dominated the scene, a little over half a century of conflict brought the Moghul Empire to its knees.

LADY SALE'S AFGHANISTAN *by Florentia Sale*—An Indomitable Victorian Lady's Account of the Retreat from Kabul During the First Afghan War.

THE CAMPAIGN OF MAGENTA AND SOLFERINO 1859 *by Harold Carmichael Wylly*—The Decisive Conflict for the Unification of Italy.

FRENCH'S CAVALRY CAMPAIGN *by J. G. Maydon*—A Special Correspondent's View of British Army Mounted Troops During the Boer War.

CAVALRY AT WATERLOO *by Sir Evelyn Wood*—British Mounted Troops During the Campaign of 1815.

THE SUBALTERN *by George Robert Gleig*—The Experiences of an Officer of the 85th Light Infantry During the Peninsular War.

NAPOLEON AT BAY, 1814 *by F. Loraine Petre*—The Campaigns to the Fall of the First Empire.

NAPOLEON AND THE CAMPAIGN OF 1806 *by Colonel Vachée*—The Napoleonic Method of Organisation and Command to the Battles of Jena & Auerstädt.

THE COMPLETE ADVENTURES IN THE CONNAUGHT RANGERS *by William Grattan*—The 88th Regiment during the Napoleonic Wars by a Serving Officer.

BUGLER AND OFFICER OF THE RIFLES *by William Green & Harry Smith*—With the 95th (Rifles) during the Peninsular & Waterloo Campaigns of the Napoleonic Wars.

NAPOLEONIC WAR STORIES *by Sir Arthur Quiller-Couch*—Tales of soldiers, spies, battles & sieges from the Peninsular & Waterloo campaingns.

CAPTAIN OF THE 95TH (RIFLES) *by Jonathan Leach*—An officer of Wellington's sharpshooters during the Peninsular, South of France and Waterloo campaigns of the Napoleonic wars.

RIFLEMAN COSTELLO *by Edward Costello*—The adventures of a soldier of the 95th (Rifles) in the Peninsular & Waterloo Campaigns of the Napoleonic wars.

LEONAUR

ALSO FROM LEONAUR
AVAILABLE IN SOFTCOVER OR HARDCOVER WITH DUST JACKET

THE 9TH—THE KING'S (LIVERPOOL REGIMENT) IN THE GREAT WAR 1914 - 1918 *by Enos H. G. Roberts*—Mersey to mud—war and Liverpool men.

THE GAMBARDIER *by Mark Severn*—The experiences of a battery of Heavy artillery on the Western Front during the First World War.

FROM MESSINES TO THIRD YPRES *by Thomas Floyd*—A personal account of the First World War on the Western front by a 2/5th Lancashire Fusilier.

THE IRISH GUARDS IN THE GREAT WAR - VOLUME 1 *by Rudyard Kipling*—Edited and Compiled from Their Diaries and Papers—The First Battalion.

THE IRISH GUARDS IN THE GREAT WAR - VOLUME 1 *by Rudyard Kipling*—Edited and Compiled from Their Diaries and Papers—The Second Battalion.

ARMOURED CARS IN EDEN *by K. Roosevelt*—An American President's son serving in Rolls Royce armoured cars with the British in Mesopatamia & with the American Artillery in France during the First World War.

CHASSEUR OF 1914 *by Marcel Dupont*—Experiences of the twilight of the French Light Cavalry by a young officer during the early battles of the great war in Europe.

TROOP HORSE & TRENCH *by R.A. Lloyd*—The experiences of a British Lifeguardsman of the household cavalry fighting on the western front during the First World War 1914-18.

THE EAST AFRICAN MOUNTED RIFLES *by C.J. Wilson*—Experiences of the campaign in the East African bush during the First World War.

THE LONG PATROL *by George Berrie*—A Novel of Light Horsemen from Gallipoli to the Palestine campaign of the First World War.

THE FIGHTING CAMELIERS *by Frank Reid*—The exploits of the Imperial Camel Corps in the desert and Palestine campaigns of the First World War.

STEEL CHARIOTS IN THE DESERT *by S. C. Rolls*—The first world war experiences of a Rolls Royce armoured car driver with the Duke of Westminster in Libya and in Arabia with T.E. Lawrence.

WITH THE IMPERIAL CAMEL CORPS IN THE GREAT WAR *by Geoffrey Inchbald*—The story of a serving officer with the British 2nd battalion against the Senussi and during the Palestine campaign.

Milton Keynes UK
Ingram Content Group UK Ltd.
UKHW010743180923
428890UK00001B/65

9 781916 535039